I AM
Broken Beautiful

Life, Love, and My Pursuit of Forgiveness

Tasha Rene'e

I AM Broken Beautiful

LIFE, LOVE, AND MY PURSUIT FOR FORGIVENESS

Editing: SynergyEd Consulting/ synergyedconsulting.com
Graphics & Cover Design: Greenlight Creations Graphics Designs
glightcreations.com/ glightcreations@gmail.com

Published by: SHERO Publishing
getpublished@sheropublishing.com
S H E R O P U B L I S H I N G . C O M

I AM
Broken Beautiful
LIFE, LOVE, AND MY PURSUIT FOR FORGIVENESS

TABLE OF CONTENTS

I AM Broken Beautiful

LIFE, LOVE, AND MY PURSUIT FOR FORGIVENESS

Tasha Rene'e

Dedication

This book is dedicated first and foremost to Abba Father. Thank you, Abba, for loving me when I was unlovable, and when my life was broken into a thousand shattered pieces. I have learned that it does not matter how broken I could have ever gotten. Your Hands would always be there to mend me back together better than I could ever have imagined. You have truly given me the most beautiful exchange.

To that sweet little girl Tasha, and all the sweet and precious girls and women that are holding it together in brokenness in their very own special way. Whether you are free from the brokenness of your past or just getting started, but do not know where to turn; I dedicate my life's work to you. You are so much more powerful than you know, and you are worthy beyond your wildest imagination. You are deserving of healthy love and relationships, not based on trauma bonding, but healed, healthy, and whole and this includes the one that you have with yourself first. You may have been broken by life's happenings, and you too may still feel shattered, but Beloved, you are Beautiful, and no one can steal that from you any longer. I pray that you make a firm decision to no longer live a life of defeat. I pray that you no longer allow the voices of your past to scream louder that your present and your purpose. My sincere prayer for you is that you too, find your *freedom* somewhere on these pages.

To my sweet girl, Jaidan Gabrielle, I thank Abba Father for you daily. I may not have shown it to you consistently because of my very own brokenness, however, you have no idea of just how big of a blessing that you are and how you saved my life in so many ways. To have never known "unconditional love" from a human perspective. Yet, this is exactly what you have given to me. I may not have gotten it right all the time, and I know that I failed in areas that I wish I were stronger in. But Jaidan, I would lay down my entire life for yours. I made a vow in my heart when I found out that Abba Father had kept His Promise to me and had blessed me with the most precious gift of you, that I would love you, protect you, never abandon you nor harm you with my hands and certainly not with my words. My arms will continue to be a safe place for you because you, my darling daughter, have my whole heart for my whole life. Mommy loves you unconditionally, always, and forever. "You are my Sunshine. My ONLY Sunshine". Mi Tortuga.

To my beautiful husband, DJ, thank you. Thank you for the life's lessons that have continued to make me stronger and better, not only as a wife, but as a woman. I know that we have had more than our fair share of turmoil, pain, and tragedy, yet somehow, it did not break us as individuals. Our relationship has not been one that has been *easy* at all, but I thank Abba for trusting me with the process and the trouble because it produced something in me and forced me to grow and it pushed me deeper into my purpose. I appreciate you for taking on the responsibility of raising our daughter and loving her unconditionally. My prayer for us is that our deepest pain becomes our greatest victory. My Little Monkey, I love you and I always will…

~Tasha

Introduction

This book is about my personal journey to healing and being made whole, not perfection. It is about being open and truthful about the deep things that I masked to cover up what needed to be unveiled to be who GOD has created me to be. It is raw, uncut, and frankly, straight with no chasers. I have been rejected, abandoned, mishandled, misused, and misunderstood. I am choosing to not hide anymore, physically, emotionally, mentally, or spiritually. It has been painful, and the road to this place has not been a walk in the park. Deliverance, healing, and restoration is not easy nor a pretty journey to travel, however, it is the place where new life begins, and the shattered places of my past can no longer hold me. Heart work is Hard work!

It might make some squirm a little in their seats, and some will be made uncomfortable. Some will clutch their pearls and may walk away. I am 100% okay with that. It has been the story of my life. Some will take offense, but then there are those who will finally take a deep breath and exhale in a place of liberty for the very first time.

This book is written for them. It is written for YOU.

I am no longer looking for the approval of people at the expense of denying my Divine Purpose. I am not writing to appease the masses nor am I in need of validation. I am not writing this book to just "tell a story", I am on an assignment. My Kingdom Assignment is to set the captives *FREE*.

Free from the bondage of rejection, abandonment, hopelessness, depression, anxiety, suicidal thoughts, and any fears that have attempted to sabotage the purpose and plans that GOD has for your life. Freedom from the lies of trying to convince everyone else that everything is great when you are literally dying on the inside; but because you have been taught to "save face" the deeply rooted issues that you have attempted to run from your whole life haunt you like nightmares on a regular basis.

This book is all about what Broken Beautiful looks like. Again, not perfection. I still have issues and I am a continued work in progress, being perfected daily. Yes, it was birthed out of the pain of my past, but it is the absolute best version of a beautiful exchange… Beauty for Ashes.

This is my testimony to God's grace and His loving-kindness, the evidence that He can, and He did take the most jacked up, sinful, insecure, broken mess, and made a beautiful masterpiece.

This is my heart laid open before you. Unashamed and unmasked. Unapologetically Tasha. My prayer for you is that you are encouraged, inspired, empowered and that you find your healing and wholeness in the same place where I found mine… In the arms of Our Savior.

"I Am Broken Beautiful", the title of this book, was spoken by Abba to me when I was invited to a Women's Ministry as the keynote speaker. I had been wrestling with and pondering over what I was going to share with the ladies that would be a powerful Word. Something that would get them all hyped up and ready to take off running! I had so many ideas in my head about what to do and even who I was going to minister on from the Holy Scriptures. I could tell them about Ruth and how God blessed her with Boaz and how "the same field that she gleaned from she became the owner of". Or I could speak about Esther, "you have been hidden but you were chosen for such a time as this". I could go on and on, however, to my surprise, I was led of Holy Spirit to research broken plates.

"Broken plates, Lord. You want me to research broken plates? What do plates have to do with empowering women in the Word? Okay, I'll research broken plates on Google".

In my research, after a few days, I came across the word "kintsukuroi". I clicked on the link to open the description and there was a beautiful photo of a vase that had obviously been broken, however, it was glued together using gold as a filler in the cracks. Its definition is, 'Kintsukuroi (n.) (v.phr) "to repair with gold"; the art of repairing pottery with gold or silver lacquer and understanding that the piece is more beautiful for having been broken". (Kintsukuroi: The Japanese Art of Embracing Broken and Flawed Things, Pinterest, Pottery, Japanese pottery). There was an article attached that ministered to the deeply rooted brokenness and pain in my own life, and somehow, 'broken plates' could tell my life's story of how I may have been broken, but I was beautiful in the hands of The Potter. This is the article from www.vikramkamboj.com titled, *Kintsukuroi: The Japanese Art of Embracing Broken and Flawed Things*.

"Are you someone who recognizes beauty in broken things? Do you embrace damaged things? If yes, then 'Kintsukuroi' will not seem foreign to you.
Unnatural it may sound but Kintsukuroi or Kintugi is the Japanese art of restoring broken pottery and ceramic objects with lacquer. In layman language, it's an 'art of broken pieces'.

Sometimes referred as 'golden joinery' or 'golden repair', the technique is used to repair broken pottery with special lacquer fused with gold, silver or platinum. You often hear people saying, "We should see a glass of water half full than half empty". This artwork is somewhat based on the positive mindset of Japanese people who consider breakage and repair as an object's history rather than keeping it behind the veil.

Where Kintsukuroi came from?

Not only is this Japanese art interesting but the story of 'how it came into being' is also very appealing. Old sources say, in the late 15th century Japanese sent a broken Chinese tea bowl to China for repairs and the end-product he got had metal staples. It looked so ugly that Japanese craftsmen looked around for something more artistic and beautiful.

Their curiosity and enthusiasm marked the birth of Kintsukuroi, the art of repairing broken pottery. It's said they were so pleased with the art that they deliberately smashed expensive pottery so that it could be mended with seams of gold. Strange but it's true!! With a 500-year-old history of golden joinery, the Japanese craftsman do not toss the broken pieces in the trash (like us!) but bring them together to get a product with an enhanced aesthetic appeal and artistic value.

Wabi-Sabi and Kintsukuroi: Both are interwoven.

How did you feel the last time you dropped your ceramic bowl that split into pieces? I'm sure you must have been shocked and annoyed.

Unlike you (and me obviously!) wabi-sabi is a philosophy that "finds beauty in broken and flawed things." While Western people consider broken objects as value/money lost, Kintsukuroi practitioners place their trust in never-ending consumerism that comes from restoration.

The 'golden joinery' does not convey replacement but values marks of wear by its use.

Kintsukuroi: Resurrecting someone from the dead

Kintsukuroi art lovers utter believe in awe, reverence and restoration can be easily portrayed through their rationale for keeping an object around even after it fell apart and then drawing attention to its cracks and repairs.

It's as if 'resurrecting someone from the dead' and simply taking breakage as an event in the life of an object instead of considering it it's end. So, Kintsukuroi reincarnates the object that would otherwise end up being in trash. This Japanese art form is not something spiritual but is a way of embracing the flawed object that looks more beautiful than the original product."

WOW!! Right, I know. My mouth was wide open, but my heart was even more intrigued that the Lover of My Soul would steer me to research broken plates to minister to me in such a profound way that set me free!

Yahweh truly takes the most foolish things to confound the wise. The words, *"reverence and restoration can be easily portrayed through their rationale for keeping an object around even after it fell apart"*, and *"it's as if 'resurrecting someone from the dead' and simply taking breakage as an event in the life of an object instead of considering it it's end. So, Kintsukuroi reincarnates the object that would otherwise end up being in trash."*

WHEEEWWWW... HE would not throw me away even though I was so broken! HE could breathe NEW LIFE into me!! Not only are the plates more beautiful because of their brokenness, but they are also of more value. Abba was teaching me that when placed in the refiner's fire I would come forth as "pure gold" and I could be used for the Master's use and He would take my broken pieces and put me back together to be on display as a Masterpiece for His Glory!

In reading this article and while sitting down in His presence, I began to weep and worship, and His sweet voice said to me, "Tasha, My Daughter, you may be broken but you are beautiful."

So, here it is… **"I Am Broken Beautiful."**

Her Story

… I somehow always wanted her to protect and save me…
Wasn't it her reason for living, to protect her family? Wasn't it her reason for living, to stop the hurting? Wasn't it her reason for living, to not allow the pain to begin in the first place? Wasn't that her reason for living?

"How could you be so cold, so filled with malice and hatred, so judgmental, so absent, and so insecure? Why were you not a voice for me? Where was my security? Where was my stability? Where was my love? Where were "YOU"? I hate you! I hate you for hurting me. I hate you for causing me pain. I hate you for creating my scars. I hate you for being the reason the tears soaked my pillow in the midnight hours. I hate you for having me. I hate you even more for the prayers I had to pray! I should have never had to pray to be saved from YOU! I should have never had to pray for the pain, both physically and mentally, the sorrow that consumed my soul, the deeply embedded wounds from your hate that you spewed on me, and the tears to STOP!

I was only a five-year-old baby! Why didn't you help me? Why did you hurt me? Why did you beat me? Why did you throw hot food on me? Why did you punch and hit me in my face and leave bruises on my little body? Why did you let him in? Why did you let him bathe me?

Why did you let him touch me? Why did you hate me? Why, Mama? Why?"

I had endured the physical and mental abuses of her, now I can't escape the sexual abuse of him... "Jehovah! Jehovah!

JEHOVAH GOD ALMIGHTY! HELP ME"???

"Who is this Jehovah that I read about? That I pray to? Why is HE not helping me? What did I do? Why does my HEAVENLY FATHER not step in when I don't have my earthly daddy to protect me? Doesn't HE see what they are doing to me? Why you HE allow them to hurt me, Abba? Why, Abba? Why? Why isn't anybody helping me? Even those that knew, why wouldn't you help me?"

This is MY story...

Chapter 1:
Life: In the Beginning

Some little girls grow up playing with dolls and in their mother's makeup. Loving to play dress up, while Mommy teaches her to polish her nails, keep house, cook and how to be a little lady. Picking out prom dresses together. Some little girls grow up with aspirations of attending the University of their choice. Building successful careers, dreaming of their very own fairy tale wedding someday, and having a loving family of their own. Some little girls have parents and grandparents that were just proud to call them their own. But most importantly, some little girls get to hear from their parents, "I love you" and feel a warm hug or a kiss on the cheek. I was not "some little girl".

For me, or at least my earliest memories, life as I would know it began around age 4. I grew up with my mom and my sister. My mom was an incredibly angry woman most of the time that I remember. Do not get me wrong, we experienced fun times together, but the troubled times outweighed them. My mom seemed to me that she would be happy one minute and then sadness and anger would take over her. I thought growing up that she was just "mean".

Most of the memories of my childhood, the time I was in my mom's custody, are filled with horrible pain and deep sadness. I remember being yelled at, hit, and having things thrown at me including a frying pan of hot eggs straight from the stove. The iron that she burned me with and the roller skates that she used to beat me. My mom would hit me with and throw anything that was close to her. I can remember, to this day, the many brutal whippings with belts that would leave bloody whelps on my tiny little body's olive skin because when she would beat me, she would be in such a rage and seemed to snap as if she were really trying to kill me. I received beatings for just being in the house. Not that I was even a bad child. I was a passionate reader and always made a good report card.

I certainly was not a sassy mouth child. I was scared to life of this woman. I knew not to do anything "bad". I did everything in my power to be and do "good" and that still did not keep her from attacking me. If she walked in the apartment angry, it was on. I could bet my life that she was going to take her frustrations out on me.

A mother's job is to feed, clothe, clean, protect and love her children. Well, this is exactly what I did for my sister. So that she never had to endure the physical beatings, I would always take the blame for anything gone wrong in our home. And again, that could be anything from an empty cup being on the carpet in the living room instead of in the sink, the beds not being made exactly the way she wanted it, the towels and bath cloths not being folded her way… ANYTHING would set this woman off.

To say that my mom had a terrible temper is to almost make a joke of just how unstable her mind was. Just to hear me breathe, I believe, would make her angry.

There was definite mental abuse that we both endured, however, the brunt of her fits of rage and hitting were always aimed at me. There were many times that she called me stupid. There were many times she told me she did not want me. I remember feeling unable to breathe when I had gotten the wind knocked out of my lungs, the stings that felt like fire from the leather belt and buckle as it broke my wet, naked skin from the force of her swings. When my mom whipped me, she always made me take my clothes off if I had on pants or a thick sweater. These beatings from her would not be for discipline. This was torture. The fits of rage always ended in pulling or snatching me by my hair, scratching me, throwing, or pushing me to cause me to hurt myself further, slapping me, just straight up "beating" me, all while screaming at me.

She just did not know when to stop. The more she hit me it seemed, the more infuriated she would become. She took all her frustrations out on me. My mom had serious problems, and a "MAN" was her fix.

My mom LOVED and NEEDED a MAN. Any man would do. My mom would be seeing a "few" men at a time. There was one that was married and 2 or 3 that were not. My mom had no trouble getting a man, it was keeping a good one that was the issue. My mom was a fighter. She was moody and would pick apart most people. She loved to fight both with her words and physically. I can say that there was one man that, I believe, she loved. He was a good man. He was kind to me and my sister and treated us well. I remember him giving money to my mom for me and my sister to go on field trips and buy us things. He would even help my mom to pay for our school pictures. However, he was married so we did not get to see him very often.

Before him, there was another man that my mom dated for a while. It had to have been for about 2 years. His name was Earl. He was extremely different because I had NEVER known my mom to ever date or even show interest to a "White" man. NEVER. As a matter of fact, the only white man that we had ever even been around in a family setting, was my uncle, my mom's half-brother. I never felt comfortable around Earl, and I was always nervous and afraid of him, but I did not know exactly why. I did not like him coming around and he just made me feel weird. I would do my best to stay far away from him. My mom, though, became fond of him. He seemed to treat my mom well. He had a decent job, had his own place, he was not married and had no children of his own. I think my mom liked the idea of having a family. He would fully decorate our apartment for Christmas with the Christmas tree filled with ornaments, the wreath on the front door, stockings, and wrapped presents for us.

This was so against my mom's religious beliefs as a Jehovah's Witness. He had fully convinced her of all the reasons why we should celebrate Christmas. However, his reasons were laden with gift giving and wanting to fill a "Daddy" role to me and my sister. This made her "love" him even more. Or at least she loved all the things he did.

It was not until about a year after "playing house" that things began to change. I believe that he knew that I could sense something about him was not right, so he began buying more things, such as the latest and greatest toys and taking us out more to dinner and the movies. He would even take his "new family", as he would call us or "his girls", to meet his parents and showing us how "loving" and caring he was. This man would even have us calling his parents our grandparents. Although, I must admit from what I can recollect in memory, his parents were kind and gentle. He made everyone think that he was our stepdad and would even say so at times, especially when he would take us to his workplace. Because he had witnessed the beatings and the mental abuse, I thought that maybe in his own way, this was his way of making up for it. Like taking us shopping at Belk and Tyler's buying us all the name brand clothes and shoes that we could have asked for and all the toys that two little girls could desire. Maybe, just maybe, he thought he was rescuing me from my mom. I know that he too was afraid of my mom when she would go off.

Most of the times that I can remember, he would leave for a few days when she would get really bad. But he had a hold on her mind too and would weasel his way right back in and things would be all lovey-dovey again. But this was only a tactical scheme though for Mr. Earl. He had a hidden agenda.

Earl was a sick minded individual and I learned this firsthand. He had begun coming into the bathroom with me and my sister when we would have bath time. This was something that he had never done in the past year. He would tell my mom that he would wash our hair and bathe us if she needed him to. I can recall him making an egg and mayonnaise concoction for our hair to use as a conditioner. This was another way that he would use to get close to us; More so me. He was scary and gross. I hated him with every fiber of my being and my mom used to spank me for not wanting him to help me bathe and wash my hair. I would cry when he touched me, and especially if we had to be alone with him. Things were getting more awful with him, and my mom was not even paying attention. Her head was somewhere in La-La Land while I am drowning in pure Hell.

I would be awakened in the middle of the night with his hands rubbing on my body beneath my nightgown. I would be so terrified that my tiny body would tremble, and my teeth would chatter. He would whisper that he loved me and that he was going to protect me and watch over me. He would tell me how pretty of a little girl that I was and that I was simply perfect. He would also tell me not to tell my mom about the nighttime visitations and the touching because she would only beat me, and she would not believe me. He was there when she had her "fits", occasionally, however, he had started to intervene. I assumed that this was his way of showing me that I could trust him. I was terrified of both these people.

Scared to tell, scared to not tell.

It was not until I was about 8 or 9 and they had broken up that I spoke out and told my maternal grandma about what had happened. I had been taken out of the home for some time by now. One day while at school, in first grade during the warm weather months, I had on a pair of shorts and while I was playing, the hem of my shorts was not quite long enough to hide the whelps from the beating with the belt. My teacher began asking me questions about what and how it happened and because I was terrified to answer, they eventually contacted Child Protective Services. I was removed from my home and sent to stay with my grandma.

That night I told my grandma about Earl and what he had been doing to me. She confronted my mom that same night and my mom became engulfed with fury. Immediately she started screaming, crying, yelling, and cussing like I had never heard. The crazy thing is, none of these emotions nor her rage were towards Earl nor what he had done. Instead, she was pissed with me for trying to break her and Earl up. She called me a liar and said that I was ruining her life. She said that I was only trying to ruin her "happiness" and that I wanted to see her miserable without someone to love her. She called me every name in the book except a Child of GOD.

Later, my mom drove into the driveway of my grandma, took me back to her home, packed my things in a big black garbage bag, all the while yelling at me and cussing me and hitting me every chance that she got close enough to me. Then, she threw the bag on the lawn outside of our apartment. As I was walking down the stairs, crying and sheer panic taking over my body, she threw my roller-skates at me as hard as she could, hitting me in the center of my back. All I heard her say was, *"Get the fuck out"*! She screamed to the tops of her lungs. *"I hate you. I hate the day you were born"*.

Remember when I said in the beginning that the physical abuse was worse at that time? Now, I truly know that scars will heal, and they do, the pain stops, but those "words" live forever!

Now, at age of nine, I am in counseling at school and my counselor, Ms. Susan Farmer visits with me regularly. I have now been permanently taken out of my mother's home and guardianship has been given to my maternal grandmother. Before this, there was a short amount of time that my biological father had taken me from my mom, but because they had not established custody legally, she was able to come to Hampton and take me away.

I wished so many years that she had just left me there. Fast forward a few years to by the time my sister was 11, both she and I were living in Hampton with my paternal grandparents. My mom had also signed over her parental rights of my sister. In my opinion, my mom should have signed those documents many years ago. Honestly, I felt that she should have never had children. Now that we were no longer living with her, things were so much better.

Chapter 2:
Hampton

Now we are staying in Hampton, Virginia with our dad in a home with our loveless grandparents; loveless that is, to my sister and me. See, we are my mother's girls, and she was and would have never been their choice for a daughter in-law. Her skin was a little too "white", and she did not come from money, nor did she have a college degree or even a high-school diploma. Her mother was a "white" woman and considered ghetto and poor white trash because she lived in public or Section 8 housing. Yet both sides of my family were all active "Brothers and Sisters" in the Kingdom Hall as Jehovah's Witnesses. That, however, did not matter in the least little bit. To them, my mom was never good enough for this family nor would she ever be. So, we were treated like not only did we not belong, but like we were not even accepted. I had heard it said quite a few times, "these are my white cousins", as if we are not of the same bloodline and ethnicity.

We are all mixed races on this side of my family; however, the complexion of our skin is light. My complexion is more olive toned than my sister. Her skin is fair, and she is blue eyed. Although my complexion is slightly darker than my dad's, I am still my mom's child, and nothing would change that. Even though we look just like my dad's family, we are still a product of everything that they are against. We not only knew it, but we also felt it. So much so, that we were not taken shopping with the money that we received monthly from the government for being in their care. We had to fend for ourselves. Most of the clothes that were bought for us were from thrift stores. I was granted the honor to have my cousin's things that she no longer wanted. We were the peasant grandchildren; The ones that needed rescuing. We should have been honored and elated that we got to stay with them. We should have counted ourselves privileged to be among them and to have the last name, "Howell".

Now, this is one of the many places where I give my mom credit, we were never on welfare to pay our bills. My mom worked two jobs and was an awesome provider. She may not have loved us the way she should have or showed us affection and kindness, but she knew how to provide and made sure that we never looked like we were thrown away. She made sure that we were clean and always well dressed, even when out to play. Our hair was always combed in place and our clothes pressed and coordinated. She always made sure that we had name-brand, good-quality clothes and shoes and that we had plenty. This was her way of making up and showing love.

Now, back to our paternal grandparents. They tolerated us and gave us a place to "stay". This was never our home. Let me be clear, not everyone in my paternal family mistreated us. There were a select few.

Chapter 3:
My Dad

My Dad. Where do I begin? My dad was a 19-year-old boy when he and my mom married. She was a young and tender 20-year-old girl. The only thing that I can say is this, in my heart of hearts I believe that my dad was never taught to be a "MAN", and he was never forced or disciplined for not being responsible for being a father to his children. I am not saying that my grandfather was not a great example for him. Was my dad loved? I am sure he was loved the best ways that his parents knew how. He was very sheltered and was a mama's boy. He has never been a father to the three of us, and I believe that it is because he chooses not to, and maybe that he does not even know how. I know my mom's name and I know my dad's. I know their birthdates and where they were born. I also know that both my parents struggled.

However, I do not KNOW my parents intimately. As of this day, June 20, 2020, I do not even know where my dad lives, works, or the condition of his health. The last time that I even heard anything concerning my dad, one of my cousins, probably in 2016 or 2017, I do not exactly remember which year, reached out to me to tell me that he had a stroke. How disgusting is that, that I would have heard that from someone else because of his own selfishness? God forbid, and I hate to say this, however, if he were already sleeping in his grave, I would not know it. Another thing that is sad, is the fact that he has never met any of his grandchildren except my oldest nephew, when he was a newborn and my brother's three children. My oldest nephew is now 23. It is heartbreaking to me.

Since the writing and revision of this paragraph, I do know that he reached out to my Auntie, his oldest sister and had her contact my brother a few years ago to see him. That is how I know that he met the grands because my brother told me and sent a photo. As for me and my sister, we were not included, because we were not invited to that reunion.

This is exactly why I said, "HE CHOOSES NOT TO SEE US". I hated him for not choosing us. I hated him for not choosing ME. I was his first born. His first Daughter. I was supposed to be "Daddy's little girl". For so many years I hated him for stealing that from me.

How could someone deny their own children? Just like the feelings of hate and resentment that I had in my heart for my mom, there was a ton of hatred and resentment deeply rooted for my dad. I hated them equally.

Chapter 4:
G'Ma

Ihad no one to love, nurture, support, care or encourage me. No one to teach me how to love and I was so confused by the grandparents who had raised us two individuals in what was supposed to be a very loving, Christian religion and household. Unfortunately, this was dysfunction at its finest.

Growing up under the doctrine of Religion based solely on works, tradition, and manipulation, I always knew that there was so much more to Jehovah than I was being taught, than I could feel, and than I was being shown. I learned the teachings and doctrine of the Jehovah's Witnesses. I would, even as a small child, question my G'ma, my mom's mom, about Jesus and why his name was rarely mentioned in the ministry or at home. The only time I honestly remember the name of Jesus being mentioned, was at the end of a prayer. "In Jesus' Name".

We did, however, practice annually the Memorial Service of the Death, Burial, and Resurrection of Jesus Christ on Nissan 14 according to the Jewish or Hebrew Calendar (Communion). Other than that, there was truly little acknowledgement of the Person and Deity of Jesus Christ. I knew God's Word says that there is NO name above all names given in Heaven, on Earth and below Earth, and NO name by which a man be saved. Isn't it the confession of the mouth that "Jesus is Lord"? I was even more confused because I started having encounters with The Holy Spirit. There was extraordinarily little study of the Holy Spirit except to define it as the Comforter. I was not taught the indwelling of the Holy Spirit, only the Comfort or Helper character in which The Spirit possesses. I did not know then what I was experiencing, nor how to explain it. I just knew that I felt safe and was never afraid when this "Presence" would appear.

I too had encounters from the demonic realm. I had nightmares since I was about four or five years of age and had even been attacked physically by demons. I knew the difference between the visitations.

I would also have visions and dreams about the Holy Spiritual realm that I was never taught. I would share these things and experiences with my G'ma, and she would always say that "Jehovah" does not operate like that, and that He would never allow such things to happen. Again, I go to the WORD and there it says, "In the last days, God says, 'I will pour out my Holy Spirit on all flesh (paraphrased from Acts 2:17 NET) …You do not wrestle against flesh and blood but against the wicked spirit forces in the heavenly places (paraphrased from Ephesians 6:12 NWT) … Talk about confusion.

My G'ma was so Anti-Church and from what the WORD of GOD says, "Anti-Christ"! I know that Jehovah's Witnesses NOW call themselves Christians. However, only in the definition that they believe that Jesus is the Savior and Son of GOD and that he is "The King of GOD's Kingdom". We better not just come out of our mouths and say, "Thank you JESUS". Mess around and be wiped out and forgotten. (Since there is no Heaven for people, except the 144,000, nor Hell).

I remember being a little girl, maybe eight years old, and hearing someone say, "Bless you" when another person sneezed. I did not understand why they said that, but I liked it. It sounded kind. Now, I am sure that I had heard it many times before this day. I do not know what my eight-year-old mind began to ponder was the meaning behind it. So, the next person that I heard sneeze, which happened to be a lady in the supermarket, I said in a big voice, *"Bless you"* and I smiled so big and waved at her. She smiled back and said "Thank you sweetie. GOD bless you too". My little mind was really churning, and I was so excited because I had done a sweet thing. When we got in the car, my G'ma was not happy. She reprimanded me and said, *"We do not talk like Church people. We do not say things like that. That is not what Jehovah would want us to say. Do not let me hear you say that again. Okay?"* In my little tenderhearted voice, I replied, *"Yes ma'am."*

I could not for the life of me grasp what made her mad and how it was a bad thing when the lady smiled when I said it to her. She even said it back to me. I was so confused.

There were many things that I loved about my G'ma. She taught me to make biscuits when I was young, she would take me with her almost everywhere she went. She and I would often sneak off to Hardee's and get a hotdog together and share a fry and Pepsi. I would go out in the Field Service with her, and she would even allow me to lead some of the household conversations while door-to-door Witnessing. We would study the Watchtower and Awake magazines together. I had come to fall in love with The Holy Scriptures. I loved being with her at The Kingdom Hall and being ready to raise my hand to "comment" on the lessons that we had studied for all week and in preparation of my answers. I loved it so much that as a young adult, I would even role play as a Sister in Field Service to illustrate how door-to-door witnessing should be done. I would be graded on my knowledge of the Scripture, my ability to lead the conversation and hold the householder's attention and lastly, I was graded on my effectiveness. I absolutely loved being a Jehovah's Witness. However, once I was baptized as a Witness, on July 14, 2000, I began to have encounters with the Holy Spirit like I had never experienced before; encounters that I did not understand.

I was always being praised by the Brothers and Sisters for doing such a good job in Field Service, keeping my time, and for my attentiveness and participation in Theocratic Ministry School.

I could never understand why I was mistreated. I was a great student. I was a loving, polite, and very well-mannered child. I was well behaved, and no one ever really had to discipline me for being rude or for being disrespectful. I just knew how I was expected to act without being told.

I was the oldest child and grandchild, so I learned how to lead exceedingly early. I was extremely outgoing and genuinely loved people, especially children and the elderly.

Everyone used to call me "sweet" and "precious". I was an exceedingly kind child. I was not mean spirited nor mischievous at all. Therefore, it made it extremely difficult for me to wrap my head around what was happening to me. I wanted everyone around me to be happy and have a good time. I loved to sing and dance and just be silly.

She just could not see it, because she couldn't see "me".

I wanted everyone to love me, especially her. She was my Mom! I wanted and needed her approval. I needed her attention in positive ways. I needed her smile. I needed to feel the warmth in her eyes and in her arms. I needed her to tuck me in at night and read with me. I needed her to teach me and guide me and show me that she was proud of me. I needed her laughter and most of all, I needed her love and affection. I just needed my Mom.

The problem with desiring these things from her is that she had none of this for me. She did not know love. She did not know affection. She did not know approval. She was "ME" and I had become her past. She did to me what had been done to her by her own mother and stepfather.

I became my mom.

I became everything that I hated about her.

Chapter 5:
Love

"If I speak in the tongues of men or of angels, but do not have love, I am only a resounding gong or a clanging cymbal. If I have the gift of prophecy and can even fathom all mysteries and all knowledge, and if I have faith that can move mountains, but do not have love, I am nothing. I give all I possess to the poor and give over my body to hardship that I may boast, but do not have love, I gain nothing. Love is patient, love is kind. It does not envy, it does not boast, it is not proud. It does not dishonor others, it is not self-seeking, it is not easily angered, it keeps no record of wrongs. Love does not delight in evil but rejoices with the truth. It always protects, always trusts, always hopes, always perseveres. Love never fails. But where there are prophecies, they will cease; where there are tongues, they will be stilled; where there is knowledge, it will pass away. For we know in part and we prophesy in part but when completeness comes, what is in part disappears. "When I was a child, I thought like a child, I reasoned like a child. When I became a man, I put the ways of childhood behind me. For now, we see only a reflection as in a mirror; then we shall see face-to-face. Now I know in part; then I shall know fully, even as I am fully known. And now these three remain: Faith, Hope and Love. But the greatest of these is LOVE". (NIV) 1 Corinthians 13:1-13

My love has always been greater for others than what I had ever received. I grew to learn that maybe what I was giving was always what I was needing. I had not been taught to love, so I did what I knew. Go out of my way to please others no matter the sacrifice to me. The wanting and the desire to be loved far outweighed the pain of rejection and not receiving love. What I thought was love was only plain lust. For anyone. I knew that I loved my G'ma, my mom's mother, but it was a different love. I honestly think that I loved her because she was my G'ma and she could fill a temporary void that I needed from my mom. Not for any other reason. And I do not say this to be ugly nor cold where she is concerned. She was my girl; My G'ma. I was the only grandchild that ever called her that. It was my thing.

However, I could never seem to get past the fact that I was not ever protected by her from my mom. I felt that she somehow accepted and had come to expect my mom to behave this way. It became something that we just brushed under the rug and it was "in the past", so it needed to remain in the past. Almost like, when my mom would say, "What happens in this house stays in this house". Well, I have learned that "what happens in this house that stays in the house" will eventually break out windows and doors. It will cause the very foundations to shake because if it is not dealt with and faced, it will show up outside of the house in ways that we never imagined. Now we have got a new saying, "there goes the neighborhood" because your filth is spreading onto everyone else's lawn.

I had become silent. Not silent in that I no longer used my voice. Silent in the ways that I was learning to suppress and make mute the things that had happened to me and the names of the people were no longer impactful. I was learning to silence their voices and by doing so, I had created my own silence to the pain they had inflicted. Silent to the abuse. Silent to the rejection. Silent to the embarrassment. Silent to the scars. Silent to the shame. Silent to the guilt. Silent to the taunting and haunting of living my very own real-life nightmares. Silent to my

Truth. My silence was far louder than any screams that had ever parted my lips.

Truth is, I was just a teen girl during this time, and I wanted to escape. I had learned to be silent and "be a sweet little girl", now I needed to be numb to it. I needed to learn to survive at a whole new level. Survival meant hiding the shame of all that had happened to me. Because I was hiding all of the pain, I was also determined to no longer "feel" it. Maybe I was 14 years of age or so when I started smoking cigarettes. I would get them from my Aunties' packs or purses or even the ones that were half smoked. I was introduced to marijuana before I was in high school. The introduction to powder cocaine came around the ages of 17 or 18. Listen, I was pouring any and everything that would fit into this voided space, but nothing was filling it. It was a bottomless pit with a slow drain; it filled up and even ran over sometimes, but always drained out and needed to be refilled. I was a pretty little mess.

I had been hurt, rejected, and abandoned by every person that ever said they loved me and every person that I had ever trusted. I had been sexually molested by a disgusting pervert, gang raped by a friend with benefits and his cousins; touched and kissed on my body by girls that were my friends. I had no clue at all who I was, nor did I have anyone that was willing or able to teach me. Instead of becoming vulnerable and gullible because that was only going to kill me, I learned to become very intentional in how I would protect myself. I learned to not trust anyone. I learned not to allow anyone, including family to get or remain close to me.

My God given personality of being loving and outgoing never changed, however, I controlled who was worthy of it. And instead of being taken for granted and having my kindness used against me, I used it to my advantage. I used my outgoing, fun, social butterfly skills to manipulate. I was determined to never let my guard down to be hurt again.

Chapter 6:
Looking for Love In All The Wrong Places

I was "*looking for love in all the wrong places*". I thought attention was love. Lust was love. Being used was love. Being taken advantage of was love. Because I was sexy, they said, I would get a lot of attention. Maybe the wrong attention, but it was *attention*! I was exotic looking with my olive tanned skin and green eyes. Not many people could figure out my race and I think that drew men to me even the more because it made me "different" since not many girls looked like me and I had a cute little body to go with it. Men, it seemed, worshiped my little petite, yet seductively curvaceous body. I had grown up fast and learned manipulation incredibly early.

I found my happy place in the club scene. I loved to dance probably before I could walk well. I had impeccable rhythm and could learn the dance moves and choreography from the hottest dance videos in what seemed like seconds. Once the music came on, I was the very first person on the dance floor and sometimes the last. I was the party starter! The neon and strobe lights, the loud thunder of the bass thumping from the speakers. The smell of Chocolate Thai and Purple Haze in the air instantly gave me a high and caused feelings of sudden happiness and euphoria to take over my whole body and mood. The sounds of the African drumbeats in the genre of Reggae with the "Winding and Ticking" like we were all from the Island of Jamaica and auditioning for the next Beenie Man video.

The hypnotic and sensual sounds, the hip gyrating thrusts to sexy Reggaeton rhythms, and the beautiful people filled the room with laughter, loud singing, dancing, and chatter that one could not ever understand over the pulse of the music. It was like being transported to another world. This atmosphere was *HOME* to me.

It was the place where I came *Alive,* where I could *Breathe* and be free. I was free. The atmosphere was filled with lust and the smell of sex. The smell of Viva La Juicy dripping from my pores glistening under the lights on my beautifully sun-kissed tanned skin. My dark curly hair drenched from sweat and the humidity from the heat of passionate skin-to-skin movement to rhythmic flow in pure synchronization. I was in the zone. When I was caught up in the tempo, I would read the room and the beautiful people to look for the precise moment to captivate the room with the most erotic dance moves with my sweet little curves. I then knew I was in total control. I, for once, had figured out how to command what I wanted and I, for once felt like I held the power.

I could feel the tender subtle brushes of sweat-soaked skin against mine as they brushed by me. Yes, all bodies were touching, however, this touch was intentional; and it was also welcomed. This touch was a familiar touch that stirred the flames of lust throughout my entire body. Men loved me and women loved to hate me. I was extremely flirtatious, and I knew how to get what I desired. There was a raging hunger in me to be touched. To be noticed. I would get so caught up in the melodies, not necessarily the words, but the beat and the rhythm and the flow and I would become completely lost in my own world of fantasy. I wanted all eyes on me. I needed all their eyes on me. My main agenda was to be the only one in the room that all bets were on. The captivating music, mixed with cocaine, marijuana, Corona, all the beautiful people, the smell of lust, and the attention made for a perfect storm. Feeling the sweat dripping from the heat of my body beneath my cropped top so high that the bottom of my breasts was exposed and my tiny 24-inch waist in the high-waisted painted on jeans that accentuated my every curve, made me feel like the sexiest girl in the room.

And the girls…. All the beautiful GIRLS! The ones that hated me publicly yet were admiring and wishing to become me. These were the same girls that privately wanted to love me; to touch me; to taste me.

And these were the same girls that would sneak up to my hotel room to have their curiosity of "what it would be like" fulfilled. All this attention from dancing was like a powerful drug that would not loosen its grip nor one that I wanted to let go of. The power to seduce flowed through my veins and I needed desperately for it not to cease. The dancing coupled with drugs and sex empowered me and somehow understood me better than I understood myself. It spoke a foreign language, however, it seemed as if it was my native tongue. I felt admired and adored while on the dance floor. This was the one space that filled me and sometimes caused me to overflow.

When I was in the clubs, I began to cultivate an air of confidence that I was in total control of the entire atmosphere and even many of the people in it. I was mesmerizing and yet, only an illusion. Dancing had become my "representative". I even named her X'tasy. I was not "Tasha" when I was dancing. No one had to know my Name, because to know my name they might find out about "Me" ….

To keep the façade, I would make sure that I wore the finest things out. I shopped at Nordstrom's, Macy's, Express, Underground, and other stores that kept up with not only fashion trends, but I knew that everyone would not be wearing what I was wearing because of the cost. I have always had expensive taste and although I was in the club often, like four days out of the week, I was still classy and very lady-like. I wanted and welcomed the attention of wealthy men.

I "loved" when men complimented me on my "banging little body". It got me a ton of attention... Maybe too much. So much so that I began to attract not just men in the dancehall clubs, but dance promoters started coming to the clubs to watch me dance.... Perform rather. See, in the dancehalls there would be nights when the club owners would hold a dance competition for money. Every time this took place, I was there. I was going to be in the competition. So, when I started to win most of the events, I began to encourage other attention.

When I was on stage performing, I would imagine that I owned the world and everyone that was in it and that I was the reason they were all there. No matter how perverse and distorted it was, it was my dream! I was an entertainer and the Super Star in my own show, and I knew how to keep anyone, and everyone engaged. The club owners started asking me about dancing in other clubs; Strip Clubs... For money! The club promoters said that I could draw crowds, just based on my looks alone, but the fact that I could dance like a "Black Girl" meant that I had an even bigger advantage. I was even promised money advanced to me for coming to clubs. I not only took the opportunities: I ran full speed at them.

I lived for this. My *dream* was finally coming true. The attention that I was receiving in the dance halls was already mind blowing, and what I prepared for, but now MONEY was thrown into the mix... Now this became my true motivation. I remember my very first-time dancing in a Strip Club, I was 17. And I was not even there as an Exotic

Dancer, I only had an invitation from the club owner. He wanted me to visit the place and experience the atmosphere. See what I thought of his place and even be introduced to a few "Ballers" that would frequent the club and were known for bringing in plenty of cash. I got to experience the club and was treated like royalty while I was there. I had a few drinks bought for me, and since I loved to dance, I danced! I did not take my clothes off, but I climbed on top of a pool table and "worked" the crowd like I knew how, and before I knew it, I was counting over Two Thousand Dollars after Three songs!!!!!???? Two Grand in Twelve mins???!!! I was hooked! All I had to do was dance? This was a no brainer for me. I now got to do what I LOVE to do and get paid!! This was It!! Jackpot!!!

Everybody loved me! I became a Feature Dancer, and I took on an attitude out of this world! I felt like Nino Brown from *New Jack City*, Diamond from *Players Club,* and Jennifer Lopez from *Hustlers* all at the same time. "CAN'T NOBODY TELL ME NOTHING"!!! AYYYYEEEEEEE!

See, you have got to understand, before this, I was waiting tables at an Italian Restaurant and getting paid off tips. I was also still working at Burger King. Of course, I was still getting money from men, too. But now I was making more money than I had ever seen, and I was not even 19 yet!!

I had all the materialistic things I could have ever asked for. All the attention that I could ever dream of. I was living the "life"! And the wonderful thing was, out of all the attention, I did not have to sleep with a bunch of men to get money, they were giving it to me freely on the dance floor! They were there to pay me! The truth is this…. I hated men! The only thing that a man could do for me was give me money and the attention that I "needed."

I was addicted to the attention and the money. In fact, during this time of my life, I had become so infatuated with women. I loved beautiful women, too!

Chapter 7:
Familiar Love

I had experienced my first girl encounter about the age of 15. So, when it came to seeing women from the club, it almost felt natural to me. Women were relatable to me, they understood me. Many also had their own past hurts that were so like mine. We shared the same pains and the same desires to be loved. I felt comfortable and safe being with "Me". I would not hurt "Me". Besides, who was better to love me than "Me"? I thought I loved me, so I loved women "like" me.

I was in a four-and-a half year open, bi-sexual relationship with a woman, who was a stripper from a club in Virginia. She was beautiful. Bi-racial and, like me, men loved her exotic features. We could relate in so many ways, however, it was the addiction to the attention and money that could afford our lifestyle that strengthened our bond. We both needed one another during this time. She was not as strong mentally as I was, and she was easily a follower. Where she cared about what others thought of her, I could care less. She was gentle and soft spoken and could be intimidated easily, which was one thousand percent the opposite of me. I was very bold and extremely cocky, I loved this lifestyle, and would fight in an instant if backed into a corner. I was not a pushover at all. Not in an unruly manner, or obnoxious… I just knew what I wanted, and I did not mind saying so, nor did I lay down when it came time to stand up. We were both so amazing and confident, yet still so insecure in our own broken ways.

So as for the men, they were good for the money, the trips, paying the bills, shopping, allowing me to "live the life" that I desired. I loved the adoration and the attention that I got from them. The unending compliments and how it seemed that they had a desire to see me "taken care of". Almost Fatherly you know? I loved being the center of it ALL. I had never committed to anyone, nor did I want to at this time. My only loyalty was to Tasha! Me.

I was chasing paper and scheming on who I could take advantage of next. Gold digger? Call it what you will. I was getting money. Besides, I loved having my cake and eating it too. What I mean is, I could see whomever I wanted, when I wanted. I could not be tied down and have a "boyfriend". That would impose and hinder my flow. Because I was the shot-caller of my life, there was nothing in this world that I could not do or see if I chose to. I lived by the motto, "Get you before you get me". However, after growing up, not just mentally but spiritually, I was only "getting" myself. You see, most nights I was alone. Unless I was on a "trip" in a hotel room, I was left alone. All this attention that I talk about, how could I be alone?

Chapter 8:
Love Choices

My choice in men were the married ones. Not just married though. Married with Money. Not a little bit of money either. I went after Owners of the Businesses. Not the manager. The CEO's and COO's. And when it came to the street game, The Ballers, I was not talking to no one that was not pushing weight. The ones that I knew I could get my way with. These were easy targets and quite easy to manipulate into becoming my "Sugar Daddy". After all, they all thought that they were "the ONE". Besides, no commitments, remember? No strings attached. I was always the "trophy" girl.

Not a bad girl at all, but most surely not the girl that you took home to meet mama. At least with the married men, there was not even the option nor expectation of being taken home. Just another way that I protected myself in and from the game.

I was perfect for the clubs, the trips, the events to be shown off like a prized possession. I was great eye candy and even better for many egos and "she-gos". I was exactly every man's fantasy and every girl's dream. Exotic looking, physically fit, sexy little body that fit everything

I put on to a "Tee". Built like a brick house! Confident. Strong, yet very submissive. Ambitious. Fun; both in and out of the bedroom. Exciting. Exotic. Adventurous. Spontaneous. Well-traveled. Articulate. Educated. I held a PhD in Street Credibility. Bi-sexual and could pull the Baddest Chicks out there. Money maker and The One that knew just how to make a "Man" feel like a "King" … Even if only for one night. I was "everything" that his wife was not. I would do things that she probably never even imagined. I could fulfill all the nasty little fantasies that her husband was craving for but would die before he made mention or requested from his wife. Most of these men dreamed of being the boy toy on a "Girl on Girl" porn set.

Yes! I was "That Bitch". The One that you had, but your boys were checking for. I was The One that could have any man extend his "business meeting". I was The One on a separate flight to meet you at our secret destination. I was The One that you were sending money to. I was The One that had you paying twice the bills because you now had not only your mortgage but a townhome that you were paying the rent on. I was The One making you get up in the middle of the night to go "checkup" on something and that "something" was me. I was The One on the other end of the phone on many occasions pretending to be someone else. I was The One. I was the reason he was not at home at night. I was the reason that he could not make it in on time. I was the reason for the flowers and the make-up gifts and trips. I was the reason for the new baby, so you would stay to keep him from paying alimony and child support. I was The One. The reason that you had to pack up and leave was because he would not let me go. I was The One needing all his time because I needed him to take care of me.

He built you a home. He hid me in a rental. He gave you a family. He gave me money. He established you with a family. He furnished me with a lifestyle. I was the homewrecker and more times than not; I was The Best Kept Secret…

I was The One that did all these things, not with ill intent, not even an ounce of malice. Manipulation? Absolutely. The desperation to "feel" anything that even closely resembled the thought that someone could care about me was worth the moments when I was left alone and once again abandoned. The desperation to be loved far outweighed the pain of not knowing love. The delusional place where I felt needed, wanted, and desired gave me the tenacity and strength to "Chase the Dragon" as a heroin addict would chase their next high in search of the first. The addiction was much stronger than the exposing or the revealing of "Tasha Renee"". I was dying on the inside, and I was willing to take the chance of hurting someone else to feel anything remotely close to love.

In no way am I proud of this lifestyle nor the terrible choices that I made. These were not mistakes; these were deliberate choices. I know I was wrong. I am not proud of any of this, in fact I find it repulsive and disgusting. On the same token though, I understand the brokenness of a woman that would choose to be a side chick or a married man's mistress; I have been both. There is nothing, and I do mean nothing, that ends well in living this way. Whether you get caught or not, whether you get to reminisce over the years about all the "fun" that you had, whether you enjoyed the excitement of sneaking around and cheating, and the high that alone can be; the day will come when you have to face the truth that you hurt families. What if someone's children were affected by your piss poor decisions? What if another woman is still dealing with the trauma of being abandoned and rejected by her own husband? Maybe she stayed and they worked it out, or maybe her family was destroyed. Maybe she reacted by reaching out to someone else where she found the attention and the affection that she was missing at home...

So many what ifs and maybes. But you want to know something that really hits home? When you become a "wife" with a family and it is your husband that cheats on you, lies to you, betrays you, abandons you and your family and he gives all that he has to his side chick or mistress! Yeah. Let that sink in. See, I have been on both sides. I used to say that I have been the "quarterback and receiver" when it came to cheating, lies, betrayal, and manipulation. I know all too well about sowing and reaping.

Chapter 9:
Love Disguised as Gifts

Acommitment? I had it all from many different men. I could keep reaping the benefits of being on "stand-by" for an upcoming event, or party, or business trip, hanging out with the fellas at the after party, or just a companion on a long car ride. Maybe there to hold your hand on a short flight to have dinner in NYC. Give all of this up? The shopping sprees. The free car to drive. The rent-free townhome. All weekend clubbing. The attention. The money. The LIFE. This was life as I knew it. And from where my beginning started, with no mother to raise me, no father to protect me, and being thrown from, as my G'ma used to say, *"pillar to post"*, sleeping on folk's sofas and floors and being labeled "homeless" ... This life was living like Royalty! By now I am twenty years of age. I had expensive clothes, shoes, jewelry, and I stayed fly! I always looked like a million dollars. I kept it sexy 24/7. But I was never happy. And even more than this, I was never loved. Absolutely loved.

I thought people loved you when they bought things for you. Much like when I was in my mom's custody. The nice clothes, shoes, jewelry, toys; this to me, was exactly what "love" looked like. After all, my mom was my first teacher, so I figured that her *"I'm sorry's"* and her "*I love you's*" always appeared as nice gifts. So, I guess, in many ways, I looked for love in "things" and not in people.

My mom and dad were divorced when I was incredibly young. My mom's mother was twice divorced. None of my Aunties at the time were married, yet all had children and men in and out of their lives. My mom was a lot like me, or shall I say, I became a lot like her, because she too, dated married men. I guess the apple does not fall far from the tree, huh? The single ones that she attempted to date were garbage to my sister and me. The only man that was good to me and my sister was a married man. Maybe somewhere in my own subconscious, I felt that I would be better treated and taken care of by a married man. A married man felt safe to me. And if not; no commitments, right? Just walk away. Another reason that I took on a no commitments attitude is because I never had anyone around me to demonstrate what a commitment was. That is sad. After all, my parents never even committed to their own children.

I was reminded by The Holy Spirit that during this time in my life I did not even receive the love from GOD Himself. Truthfully, I did not know how. I knew that HE loved me. HE is GOD, however, because I had never known what tangible "true" love looked like and how it was demonstrated, I could not receive it. If I could not receive what I could touch and feel with my natural hands, how could I begin to touch and feel with my heart and by my Spirit what I could not see? I did not know what to look for. I had no idea how to love nor to be loved.

So, about me being "The One", that girl, truthfully, she is not at all "Who I Am" today and the "Woman that I Am Still Becoming", yet she helped to develop me. She was then and forever will be necessary. She is the star in my "book" that will never be forgotten, nor will I water down her existence, nor remove her voice from the script. For so many years I absolutely hated her. I hated where she came from and her parents. I hated everything about her, including her name; Tasha Renee'. However, I have grown to know that her season and timing were impeccable. I have grown to fall in love with her and no longer see her as my adversary, but more like a little girl that indeed needed a Savior. She was screaming all those years, and no one heard. When I say her name today, I say it proudly, because I say "my" name. I love her because no matter how it may seem, and no matter how dirty and disgusting it all was; everything that has gotten her to this place was all ordained by GOD Himself and He has never been ashamed, nor embarrassed to call me His Own.

Chapter 10:
Love Reversal

So now, I have decided that I no longer want to be "that girl", rather, I do want a commitment. I do want a home. I do want someone to call all mine. I want everything that I have ever imagined and hoped "love" could be. More than anything, I want to be a mommy someday. I want to be a good wife and not a "trophy girl" any longer. I want more for "me". So, I traded my townhome in Hampton, Virginia and the lavish hotel stays and the first-class flights and the cars and the events. The trips and the shopping and most of the clubbing and lastly, my bi-sexual lifestyle, for my then, best friend's grandmother's sofa. I was living out of my suitcases and bags.

Chapter 11:
A Fool in Love

Something happened? Yes. Something happened. So, after the trophy girl lifestyle and moving in with my old best friend at her grandmother's house I am ready for a change. Now, I am still clubbing, and I am still an exotic dancer… I am still "In Da Club" …. I joke now when I give my testimony that I had a 50 Cent anointing (The Rapper that recorded the song "Da Club") … I was always in the club. From Thursday night until Sunday morning…You could find me in da club! Okay, okay. I am moving on.

Then, I found, "The love of my life." OMG!! I just knew that I had found my soulmate. My everything. The finest, sexiest, black, dark chocolate man that I had ever had as mine!! He attended a private party the night that we met. I was paid to dance there. It was by no means, not even remotely close to the club scenes that I was used to, but hey, it is still money and I still need it. I noticed him when I first walked through the door. We came through the back door of the house, and he happened to be in the hallway where I had to pass. There were only two of us dancing this night, it was a small bachelor house party. Like I said, nothing to write home about. I believe that we spoke in passing. We caught eyes for a moment. Nothing crazy like fireworks or anything.

After the dancing was over and we got paid, we were kind of hanging out, eating with the guys, and cutting up. Just having fun. A few blunts were being passed and the music was still jumping, so even though I am fully dressed, I am still dancing. He had sent his boy over to get my attention. Now, as giddy as that reads coming off the pages, that is not at all the persona that I gave. I am a trophy girl, remember?

I know I said I want the commitment; I know all that I have said and written, however, I'M STILL BAD!! I'M STILL MY OWN SHOT-CALLER!! I STILL GOT IT!! I did not say that I fell off because I was not living in the shadow of married men any longer. I was *keeping* it real sexy. Yes, and I continued to smoke weed and cigarettes, but nothing more than an occasional drink. Stay with me. At this point, I wanted my "own". I wanted to be "wifey". Okay, so him sending his boy over, was "supposed" to happen. I was the sexiest little thing in the place. And because my mouth was so slick, and I invented "game", the first words out of my mouth were, "If he needs a mouthpiece, I'm not interested"!

So, after his boy walked away, maybe 10 mins later, he came over to introduce himself. He had a great "mouthpiece" and a very intellectual conversation. And on top of that, he was one of Brooklyn's FYNEST!! A Brooklyn Bad Boy!! Although the married men that I had seen in the past were "Suits" and beautiful, there was always a mystery to the Bad Boy persona that was a bit of a turn on. He had swagger. He was as smooth as the chocolate on his skin, and this one had "Game". Now, "Game recognizes Game" and I had written a novel on game and how to be a playa, (We all have our book) …. I had a game for *DAYS*, but I loved the game and the way that he played, and I was eager to be on the team. Truth be told, I was a Sucker. Bona-fide USDA certified FOOL!!! But I was a fool for his "love"; only to find out that I was in total lust!

Chapter 12:
Love: Ignoring the Warning Signs

Married to my Brooklyn Bad Boy! *"He"* will remain nameless throughout this season for legal purposes… So, where were we… After meeting him and considering myself in love, I wanted to be married. I wanted to be a wife, but most importantly, I wanted to be HIS wife. In the year of 96 we met. In the year of 98 I decided, with his support, that I would no longer be in the clubs, nor would I be dancing or stripping. In 97 he encouraged me to go back to school to get my GED, and he supported me. After I got my GED, he supported me in my decision to continue attending Community College and I received an Associate Degree in Justice Studies for Juveniles. In between the GED and Associate Degree were three years, because I started in Business Administration only to find that I hated it because of the math courses.

I struggled with math throughout school and needed tutoring. I was always able to pass, that is how I kept good grades, even Honor Roll for many years. Math and I did not get along. Funny to a girl that loved counting MONEY! I could do that "math" all day. So, between 97 and 2000, I decided that in 98 that I genuinely wanted this relationship to last, so I started praying. I do not think that I had done that in many years. Maybe I did, I just do not remember. I do not remember making GOD a priority.

For the first time, in many years, not only did I begin praying, but I really started seeking GOD for myself. Remember, I learned to pray at a very youthful age, I had encounters with The Holy Spirit as a young girl, so I knew "how" to pray, or at least talk to GOD. I was raised in Religion. I was taught to pray and study the Bible. These things were my foundation. Even if it was taught from a religious and not a relational standpoint, I knew Jehovah to be 'The Creator of all things" and I knew Jesus as "My Savior". If I knew nothing else, I knew that there was Only One GOD that I pray to in the Name of Jesus.

What I was seeking though, was something "different" from GOD. While I was seeking GOD, I got the courage to tell him my heart's desires. To rekindle and build a relationship with GOD, but to also start a life with him as husband and wife. I remember praying for nearly a month, daily, about getting married and repenting for committing deliberate sin by fornication and then one night, right in the middle of my prayer and cries, I said to GOD just this plain…

"I am no longer going to ask your forgiveness for my deliberate sin. This is no different than a child who sneaks out of the house only to get caught and promise not to do it again. Then the next night do the same thing, only this time to get a spanking and promise to never do it again. Only to do it again. Get a spanking, get the windows nailed shut and again promise to never do it again. It is a lie, and I will not have you turn a deaf ear to me, and I will not grieve the Holy Spirit to have no opportunity for forgiveness. So, Heavenly Father, Jehovah, I will no longer ask you to forgive me for having sex with this man, when I know and so do you, that I'm going to do it again tonight. So, GOD, if it is your will, please allow me to marry him and I will never ask your forgiveness of this again. In Jesus' Name, Amen."

Because I was a babe in the Revelation of the WORD, and did not really *know* Jesus intimately, much less have what I would consider a relationship, the very next month at 10:30 pm at the magistrates' office in the County Jail on April 6, 1999, we were married. He had mentioned to me that he too wanted to be married, so we had already applied for our marriage license and knew that we had to be married within thirty days or we would have to reapply. I thought this man was the best man on planet Earth. I worshipped the ground that he walked on, even though the flags were there from the very beginning: the red flags, and they were flying high.

The red flags, or warning signs of an abuser and narcissist were obvious. They were disguised though as "love". I looked at the jealousy and controlling as being cute and his way of demonstrating to the world that I was his. Before we got married there were other women. A few women to be exact. I had found naked photos, and not just naked photos, I mean photos where he would cut the photo to remove the heads of the women to hide their identity. Photos of his fingers penetrating these women. Night gowns, women's razors and Bath and Body Works' shower gels and lotions hidden in the spare room closet. Love letters written to him from the best friend of his ex in New York City. Video recordings of him and other women. Even the photo of a seventeen-year-old that he was messing around with that worked at Burger King. Not to mention the other seventeen-year-old that he was getting from the bus stop and hiding her mom's van, who was supposed to be a Pastor, behind my house so that it would not be repossessed.

He was even wearing her initial necklace with a "N" on it and told me he "found it"! The hotel receipts from North Carolina when he was supposed to be in New York City, I could go on and on. When I would confront him, I would get either the abuser or the narcissist response. Meaning we would either get into huge verbal arguments where in turn he would start to fight me, or I would get the sad victim. And when I say "fight", I mean physical fist fighting. At that stage in our relationship, I would fight him back with all my strength. In the response of the narcissist, he would make me feel like it was some type of closure that he needed because he did not "break-up" the right way as if there was an all-of-a- sudden, newfound wave of integrity and awareness that he had come upon him. His rationale was that he did not want to lead anyone on by having them not know that he was with me... Since he was wanting to marry me and make me his wife, I had no worries. Everything in me said, "RUN!! GIRL, RUN!!"

The first time that he shoved me and laughed it off; I should have been long gone. I will never forget the look that was on his face the very first time that he snatched me. I was so startled because this was before the fighting, and I had not seen any aggression from him. We were quite a few months in. I was leaving to go to Virginia, and he was supposed to be going to New York City for the week to get his remaining belongings. As I was leaving, I reminded him of the phone call that had happened earlier in the week. It was a woman on the other end when I answered the house phone. She sounded very friendly and spoke to me as if she knew me. I said to her that she must have misdialed. Immediately she corrected me to tell me her name and said,

"You must be his sister". I called him to the phone, and he played me in my face to her. He walked outside to take the call. So, when I was leaving, and I am sure that I said something slick, he snatched me. I am sure that fear showed on my face.

The feeling that rose up in my gut was all too familiar. It was the same gut wrenching, sick, nervous feeling that I would get when my mom became enraged. I could feel the lump growing in my throat making it difficult to swallow. I could feel "it" rising within me and my heart began to pound so hard in my chest that I could literally hear it in my ears. I am sure, like an animal stalking its prey, he could sense the fear and it empowered him. It was a sick and demon-like grin that crept across his lips as if to say, "I got you now". The many times that I did leave; I should have stayed away. But, in my own insecurities, and because of the shadows of my own past, I thought this was all that I deserved.

I came to learn that the one thing that he "loved" about me, would be the thing that he hated most about me and would attempt to use it to destroy me.

Who else was going to have me? Who else was going to accept my past experiences as a throw away and outcast? Who else was going to want a commitment with me when my own parents hated me? Who else was going to marry me after I was used and damaged goods? Who else was going to be accepting of me as a bi-sexual, drug using, home-wrecking stripper? Who else was going to love me? Who else was going to be around? I was far beyond broken. I was shattered. I was desperate. All I wanted was affection. All I wanted was acceptance of "Me" and not to be just a sexy little body lying in another man's bed. I wanted more. I desired more. I needed more. I longed for more. I prayed for more.

I figured because I had prayed for a husband, for this man to be my husband; this had to be God's way of answering me. Right? Was I right? Was it God's answer, or my own desires or addictions to have someone to call "mine" that I was so willing to accept the abuse, the mishandling, the misuse, the lies, the betrayal, the hurts, the pains, the rejection? I was accepting of the fact that this treatment was a result of my low self-worth. I was not worth more than I was getting. This was not the behavior for the entire 18 years; however, the damage was done. Even in the times that we were good, and they were not constant, there is always that "thing" in your mind and in your gut, that just has a way of "reminding" you. For anyone that has experienced abuse, you know exactly what that feeling is. Those triggers that have a way of shaking you awake to reality or cause you to tremble with fear. Always expecting the expected.

I was so addicted to him, our makeup sex, and my own yearning to be loved and accepted that I was willing to stay in the delusion of this relationship that I called "marriage". Even before the marriage, I still wanted to be his wife. There is such a low you get to as an abused woman, not just physically, that the only way that you see your self-worth, is through the eyes and actions of your abuser. No matter how bad it hurts, you are always doing all that you can to somehow gain their approval and there is a sickening attachment and neediness from them. I call it the "look at me" syndrome. Like that of a child. Needing validation. Any validation.

Even though we had endured more than our fair share of hard times and F-ups, I still wanted to be a mommy. I wanted to have a baby more than anything on Earth. We were having sex and plenty of it. This was our way of making up and to be totally honest, especially in the beginning, it was the only thing that we had in common. Sex was our restart button. I think it reminded us of our attraction to one another and it was the only way that I felt like I was in control. So, after years of having sex, unprotected and no birth control, we were not getting pregnant. I was really having baby fever about 3-4 years into our marriage. I expressed my desires with him, but I do not think that it was number one on his list.

After speaking with my gynecologist and trying some fertility meds and timed intercourse, to no avail, she suggested we see a fertility specialist. I planned, scheduled appointments, and started that chapter in my journey.

Chapter 13:
Love Lost

"For this child I prayed, and the LORD has granted me my request which I asked of HIM. Therefore, I have also dedicated him to the LORD; as long as he lives he is dedicated to the LORD." And they worshipped the LORD there." 1 Samuel 1:27-28

My quest to have my "love child" began with a battery of different tests. From Clomid to artificial inseminations. From surgery to egg retrieval. From IVF to miscarriage. And over again. Three surgeries, two artificial inseminations, two IVF attempts and the loss of twins.... Where do I go from here? Anger. Frustration. Pissed. Mad. Disappointed. Depressed. Worthless. Afraid. Useless. Guilty. Barren. Cursed. Ashamed.

I could finally understand if he chose to cheat on me again. Even though, to me it appeared, as if he did not want to have a baby. Maybe he did not want a baby with me. Every man wants a son, right? What man does not want his legacy? I am not sure if his coldness was because he did not know how to respond to me, or if he was somehow relieved that it did not happen. I went through years of therapy from the debilitating thoughts of not being a mommy. The suffering and pain that comes with the loss of a child. The sorrow and the shame that eats at your soul like a cancer. Who could know this pain? Who could know this type of hurt? It is one thing to feel or be betrayed and rejected by man, or people in general. It is another level of pain, hurt, rejection and shame when you feel it comes from GOD. The Creator of All things. The GIVER of life.

"The One that Created me...... Did He not know my pain? Did He know not how to fix me? Did He not love me enough to cause me to get pregnant? Did He not know that I had been through ENOUGH!! ...

"WHAT DO YOU WANT FROM ME? WHY ARE YOU PUNISHING ME? WHY DO YOU DESPISE ME SO MUCH? WHY HAVE YOU TURNED A DEAF EAR TO ME? I KNOW I HAVE SINNED AGAINST YOU! I KNOW ALL THE TROUBLE THAT I HAVE CAUSED! I HAVE SAID I AM SORRY AND I HAVE REPENTED TIME AND TIME AGAIN! ... WHY DO YOU CONTINUE TO PUNISH ME? I NEVER ASKED YOU FOR ANYTHING EXCEPT TO BE LOVED. JEHOVAH, ALL THAT I DESIRE IS A CHILD OF MY OWN. TO HAVE SOMETHING AND SOMEONE TO CALL MINE. SOME-ONE THAT WILL NEVER LEAVE ME. SOMEONE I CAN SHOW WHAT LOVE IS AND SOMEONE THAT WILL LOVE ME IN RETURN UNCONDITIONALLY. WHY DO YOU HATE ME? WHAT DID YOU GIVE ME PARENTS THAT HATE ME? WHY DID YOU ALLOW THEM TO ABUSE ME AND TO STEAL MY YOUTH AND MY DIGNITY FROM ME? WHY DID YOU ALLOW ME TO LIVE TO ONLY ALLOW ME TO BE TORTURED? WHY?"

"How many times do I have to say, 'I am sorry?' How many years will you allow me to live this way? Just kill me! Let me die! Just let me go to sleep and never wake up! I hate my life! This is no way to live. Why do You hate me so much that You would continue to take from me and allow people to destroy me?"

On that day in December of 2003, I had arrived, brokenhearted and filled with grief, at the North Carolina Center for Reproductive Medicine in Cary. I returned because I had miscarried my twins during the first trimester of pregnancy after the insemination in October when I was told that my babies were "viable". Once I had the D&C (Dilation and Curettage) procedure which included the dilation of the cervix and surgical stripping away part of the uterine lining and any residue of my unborn babies and laying on a cold, hard table for what seemed like hours, I began my drive back home on Interstate 40. I was devastated and in such deep pain. Not so much from the pain and cramping of the D&C, but the heartbreak of not being pregnant and never holding my sweet babies in my arms. The cramping reminded me that my babies no longer lived in me where they belonged. I had imagined their sweet little faces so many times. I would have the most vivid dreams of their little faces and holding them. I would lay my hands on my belly and talk to them and sing to them every day. I, for the first time in my life, felt grief.

By the time I had gotten to my exit off Interstate 95, I had become so angry that I just began to yell, cry, and wildly lash out; fully enraged at GOD. I was hurting. Like, I had never felt this level of hurt before. This pain was the worst pain of my life. There was no way possible that I could have ever even begun to imagine this kind of pain. I could not even imagine that any person could feel such agony deep down in their bones. This pain ran deep within the very core of my being. It had snatched the ability to breathe, and it literally felt like my heart had been ripped from my chest and stomped on repeatedly. I had no idea that my life could get any more painful and that the feelings of rejection and worthlessness could reach a depth within me that I didn't know existed. I had finally reached the lowest point in my life. I felt as if GOD Himself had betrayed me, too.

I could not fathom why or what was happening to me and in me. What is worse is the fact that I had to go through this process and anguish all alone. He decided not to drive me to NCCRM that day. He said that he could not take off work because he had incomplete job orders that had to be finished and closed by a certain time. In so many ways, I was relieved that he had chosen to not come with me. If he had been there, I would have had to "suck it up". Therefore, I would not have been able to express my emotions and my heart's unbearable pain.

The next week I was scheduled to see my psychiatrist for my regular weekly visits. Like I mentioned before, I was going through a lot with infertility issues. My psychiatrist was my outlet and allowed me to be as candid as necessary about my feelings and the emotions I was experiencing without casting judgement.

On this visit though, things were quite different. I was usually talkative. Even through my pain I could articulate well what I was experiencing. I did not hesitate to share with her where I was mentally, and how I was doing in my journey. However, on this day, I was quiet and reserved. I sat almost motionless, with little to no eye contact. I guess you could say that I was "zombie-like". I was mentally in the best place that could be expected, given the depth of my grief. I was grieving as any mommy that had lost a baby to death. This was all unfamiliar to me and I was devastated. I wanted to scream and throw things and fight. I wanted to drive my car into a tree and kill myself instantly! All I wanted was for the pain to STOP!!! My mind and heart were screaming so loud for help, but all that I had the energy to do was weep and mourn. By this time, there were no more tears. My soul mourned.

I had spent the past few nights on my knees in desperate prayer, weeping in travail, pouring my heart out before the Lord. Nevertheless, I was still angry, and the pain just would not cease. On a scale from 1 to 10 for pain, I was at 100 and there seemed to be no sign of relief coming to my aid. I got up from my bedroom floor, on the last night of praying, crying, mourning and begging, and I went to run myself a bath. I walked into the bathroom at the end of my hallway. It was smaller than my master bath, which was big and spacious. This space I liked more because it was cozier and felt more intimate, like that of a closet. I went in with my Bible and closed the door behind me. I turned on the ventilation fan. I loved the sound of the water running in the bath, however, once the tub was as full as I could make it without it running over, the sound of the fan was just as soothing to me. The shower curtain was a deep burgundy and gold, so when I pulled it closed it blocked out most of the light from the vanity, like blackout drapes. Leaving just enough light peeking behind the curtain to allow me to clearly read the WORDS on the pages. I got the bath water to the perfect temperature and turned the knobs on just enough so the water would flow slowly. I got in and sat down with my knees bent as if making a table with my knees. I then placed my washcloth over my knees and laid my Bible on my lap. I opened my Bible to Psalm 51. I began to read the Words in a whisper, The Restoration Prayer and Psalm of King David.

A Contrite Sinner's Prayer for Pardon.

To the Chief Musician. A Psalm of David; when Nathan the prophet came to him after he had sinned with Bathsheba.

"51 Have mercy on me, O God, according to Your lovingkindness;
According to the greatness of Your compassion blot out my transgressions.
Wash me thoroughly from my wickedness and guilt
And cleanse me from my sin.
For I am conscious of my transgressions and I acknowledge them;
My sin is always before me.
Against You, You only, have I sinned
And done that which is evil in Your sight,
So that You are justified when You speak [Your sentence]
And faultless in Your judgment. I was brought forth in [a state of] wickedness;
In sin my mother conceived me [and from my beginning I, too, was sinful].
Behold, You desire truth in the innermost being,
And in the hidden part [of my heart] You will make me know wisdom.
Purify me with [†]hyssop, and I will be clean;
Wash me, and I will be whiter than snow.
Make me hear joy and gladness and be satisfied;
Let the bones which You have broken rejoice.
Hide Your face from my sins
And blot out all my iniquities.
Create in me a clean heart, O God,
And renew a right and steadfast spirit within me.
Do not cast me away from Your presence
And do not take Your Holy Spirit from me.
Restore to me the joy of Your salvation
And sustain me with a willing spirit.
Then I will teach transgressors Your ways,
And sinners shall be converted and return to You.

Rescue me from bloodguiltiness, O God, the God of my salvation;
Then my tongue will sing joyfully of Your righteousness and Your justice.
O Lord, open my lips,
That my mouth may declare Your praise.
For You do not delight in sacrifice, or else I would give it;
You are not pleased with burnt offering.
My [only] sacrifice [acceptable] to God is a broken spirit;
A broken and contrite heart, broken with sorrow for sin, thoroughly penitent],
such, O God, You will not despise.
By Your favor do good to Zion;
May You rebuild the walls of Jerusalem. Then will You delight in the sacrifices of righteousness,
In burnt offering and whole burnt offering;
Then young bulls will be offered on Your altar." (Amplified Bible version).

The words seemed to leap off the pages, capture my heart and come alive in me. *"Make me hear joy and gladness and be satisfied: let the bones which You have broken rejoice. Create in me a clean heart, O God, And renew a right and steadfast spirit within me. Restore to me the joy of Your salvation. My [only] sacrifice [acceptable] to God is a broken spirit; A broken and contrite heart-broken with sorrow for sin, thoroughly penitent], such, O God, You will not despise."*

There were many, countless times that I had read that same passage of Scripture. In fact, it was the one place that I sought most in GOD's WORD. But, right now, in this moment of time, something strange was happening within me. It was that very night that I, for the first time, humbled myself and surrendered to GOD everything that I had left in me. All of this was taking place while still reading and crying out in HIS WORD. Immediately, as soon as I finished reading the 19th verse of that same Chapter, I heard with such clarity a voice whisper to me, *"Jaden"*. I stopped sobbing and held my breath. I quickly wiped my tear-filled eyes, sat up in the bath and petitioned GOD to speak to me again. I begged HIM to. He did not. With a sense of urgency, I gathered myself, got out of the tub to find a pen and I wrote the name "Jaidan" from my Bible, onto paper.

A few days passed, and I was doing everything that I could to hold on to every specific detail of that night. While at the psychiatrist's office for my weekly visit, I could only think of the experience in my bathroom the week before. There was a bubbling on my Spirit, like an anxious anticipation or nervousness that I could not comprehend. This feeling was like being at Busch Gardens and waiting in the line to get on the most thrilling roller-coaster. Once boarded, the coaster starts moving in a climbing position. I can hear the clicking sound of the tracks, forcing the coaster upward to the peak where the "drop" happens. But, once the coaster has reached the peak, there is a pause that builds an overwhelming anticipation. I know exactly what is about to happen; I just do not know when. My former experiences with GOD had never left me feeling this way.

After the psychiatrist and I had spoken during this visit, I simply stated to her that I appreciated all the time that she had spent with me. I thanked her for the suggestions and advice and assured her that I was grateful. I then let her know that I was going to go, and that this would be our last visit.

As I was preparing to leave, getting my purse from the seat of the chair next to me, I stood and looked at her, and with tears streaming down my face and heaviness in my heart, I cleared my throat to say, *"There is only One who knows and truly understands what I'm going through, and there is only One that can fix this".*

I walked out never to return.

Chapter 14:
Love Granted

I arrived back to work after being out for a few weeks due to the miscarriage. Because I did not have internet service in my new home yet, I logged onto the computer at my workstation and googled that beautiful name which had been spoken to me by the Voice of GOD. I did some research on the name Jaidan, the way that I would have spelled it, and found it to be a "Hebrew male child name". Its Biblical interpretation is *"Jehovah has heard, or God has given ear"*. This definition came from babyzone.com. I began crying to the point of being nearly hysterical and causing a scene. I was trying to quickly print the page, and to get off the sales floor quickly. I managed to print to the printer in the back of the store and I excused myself to the bathroom. It was not unusual that I would be having a hard time, and maybe even crying. My manager and two employees that I was close to, knew about the fertility treatments and the miscarriage. After all, it was my first day back. Maybe they figured I had become overwhelmed from the pain of the memories that blanketed me from the death of my precious babies. Therefore, they left me to myself to mourn. When I got to the printer, I grabbed the paper and headed straight for the bathroom. I was sobbing, but this time, not because I was hurting. I was rejoicing. I read the printed page, over and over again!

GOD HAD NOT TURNED A DEAF EAR TO ME! HE HAD HEARD MY HEART'S CRY! BUT BETTER THAN THAT… HE ANSWERED MY DESPERATE PRAYER! HE HAD HEARD THE DESPERATION IN MY BROKEN AND CONTRITE HEART. AND HE DID NOT DESPISE ME! HE HAD RETURNED TO ME, OR SHALL I SAY, INTRODUCED ME TO THE JOY OF HIS SALVATION FOR THE VERY FIRST TIME! My *"Jaidan Gabrielle"* was born March 2005. Yahweh had spoken Jaidan's full name to me. Because Yahweh heard and answered my prayers, HE chose her middle name as HIS Messenger. Derivative of Gabriel, GOD's CHOSEN Messenger. We serve an awesome GOD! He IS Great and Worthy to be Praised!!

Chapter 15:
Love Sabotage: 2005-2006

Now life was supposed to be so much better because GOD had blessed me, us, with this bundle of joy of a beautiful baby girl. This was not the case at all. See, by the time we had gotten to this year, 2005, so much damage had been done in our marriage and relationship, that honestly, nothing, not even the birth of our daughter could have even begun to mend the amount of physical, emotional and mental damage that existed. Nevertheless, with a weak, and completely twisted and sick mindset, I somehow thought that our daughter would be the answer to him finally falling in love with me and desiring to have a beautiful life together. Besides, we had just purchased almost six acres of land and our brand-new home the previous year. We had painted and bought beautiful furniture. I had decorated our home with love and tender care. I loved that sweet place. It was quaint and had so much personality; it was my happy place. It was my first home and I loved it. I even nicknamed her my "Doll House". It vrwas dainty yet sophisticated much like me. It was our first "home" together. Since we had only rented in the past, I was sure that living in the new home and certainly being blessed with a beautiful healthy baby girl would cause things to get better between us. It did for a while. A short while.

A "hot minute" while. It was only a matter of time that he was back with his ex-girlfriend that he dated in high school. I had, unfortunately, become awfully familiar with her. She always seemed to just "appear" in our lives because she was his main side chick. The one that he had a history with, so she was easy for him to run back to. In fact, they made it convenient for one another, even though she too, at the time, was married, he was always welcomed with open arms. She knew exactly who I was. Somehow, she knew where I worked and even when I was offered a transfer into the town in which she lived. I guess it had to be made known so that she would not "accidentally" run into me, or I would not accidentally run into *them*. In 2006 I had befriended a gentleman that worked in law enforcement that I had met through my work. I worked in the wireless industry, so it was not unusual to meet new people almost daily. My job was just off Interstate 95, so there were always new faces. It was casual conversation at first, and then he started to delve into my personal business. Asking subtle, but clever questions.

He obviously knew who I was, but I did not have a clue to who he was. The town that I worked and lived in was the town in which my husband grew up and where his family was originally from. So, it would not be strange that people that saw us together would know me as his wife. It is a small town; you know, the kind where "everybody knows everybody". So, of course, when the gentleman started asking questions, I genuinely thought that he was trying to get to know *me,* not build a case file to bestow information upon me. I guess after a few months passed and he had become more comfortable in his chit-chat with me in my workspace, he just asked me, out of the blue, if I knew, *her.* I looked at him very sternly and said, "I do. Why do you ask"?

My initial thought was that this man was pulling some ole slick*ish,* like he was throwing her up in my face. Like I was being set-up for some mess. He went on to tell me that he and she were friends, and he knew that she was seeing my husband and that she had been seeing him for a while. As in YEARS. It was an OFF/ON relationship with them. Now, this information was of no surprise to me, whatsoever. However, the fact that someone, anyone, would approach me with this mess, had me vexed.

So, I flipped the script on him. I wanted to know all that he knew so that I could catch the two of them together. We exchanged numbers to take this conversation from my workplace and into a more private area. In no way did I want anything to interfere with my money, so as much as I wanted to know more, this was not the place to hold conversations at length and allow any conflict. I had a particularly good paying corporate job in wireless sales, and I loved it. Besides, I had been with this company now for 5 ½ years and had earned recognition for my sales performance over the years. I was one of many top producers in our region and rewarded most for providing excellent customer service. So, work had to remain work and nothing personal.

I, must admit, I became quite inquisitive of just how much this gentleman knew about their affair and why he felt comfortable divulging this information as if it was a casual conversation. Even though I had my doubts and felt like this had to be a set-up, I also felt as if I finally had someone that was in my corner because no one would have ever believed that my *Mr. Prince Charming* was a lying cheating womanizer! Especially not his family that hated me from day one because my skin was a little bit too light for their taste. Any who... Now, let me be really clear, I was not at all wanting to catch them with the hopes that my husband would feel sorry and come crawling back begging my forgiveness. Nah, the marriage had been over. We only had legal documentation that stated that we were still married.

I wanted to approach her because of the little stunt that she had pulled, a few weeks prior, by showing up at my job to be funny or cute. I assumed that she thought that because I was on my job, and it was a corporate setting where I wore business suits and stilettos and drove that little Mercedes-Benz, that I would not check her. She found out differently when she moved to exit the building and I caught her between my desk and the double glass doors. The only thing that I said to her that day was, "*Bitch, you might play these silly little games with these other women of the men that you are fuckin', but let me promise you this, I will throw your ass through that glass door and never bat an eye. Do not ever show up on my job again. This silly shit just got really personal.*"

I will never forget the look on her face nor the face of the store manager who just so happened to be one of her homegirls. I left there that day, once I had closed the store, and I immediately called my newfound friend. I needed someone that could talk to me logically. I could not and would not talk to my husband. He would only defend her and try to convince me that I was the one "making an ass of myself" and reading more into it than it was.

I was ALWAYS over-analyzing EVERYTHING when it came to him, even when I was wrongly treated. He could be dead wrong, caught in the act, and I would still be jumping to conclusions and not know what I saw. He was always right. Never guilty and always the victim. So, I got my friend on the phone and I began to tell him what had happened and the words that I spoke. He came to my defense right away and made me feel like I had done only what any rational person would do in that situation. He allowed me to vent, be angry and get it all out. Crying and all. I was so angry. Then suddenly, he began to speak to me gently and console me. I had never had anyone around to console me. To make me feel as if they cared enough about *me* to care about how I was feeling. He did not even know me well. He knew my name, my husband, where I worked and my phone number. I suppose too that because he was a law enforcement officer, I felt safe talking with him. Not to mention the kindness that seemed to exude from him and the pure joy that leaped in my heart every time he spoke to me from that day forward. Truthfully, everything about this man made me feel safe. For the first time ever, I felt SAFE.

Chapter 16:
Love Assaulted: 2006

An early morning, around 6:30 before the alarm went off, in August of 2006 began this way...blood-curdling, horrific screams from the excruciating pain in my head from his closed fist blows. My body being slammed violently to the floor of my bedroom and then being dragged forcefully by my hair. The fierce punching and the repeated stomping to my body as I did everything that I can to cover my face and head from the brutal assaults that were inflicting serious pain. With every hit I would gasp for my breath. I was not even awake when the attack first began. I could not even, nor did I have time to think about what was happening to me. I could hardly catch my breath between the sharp pains that I felt surging through my body like electricity; feeling like someone was stabbing me with a knife. I wanted to fight back, but I couldn't. I was too terrified. I honestly think I was in shock and my head was pounding with unbearable and unimaginable pain. I remember wanting to open my eyes, but I was so afraid of what I might see. Maybe I was in survival mode and did what I could to cover my face. I was confused and whenever I did open my eyes the room kept going black. The ringing in my ears was deafening. I didn't even recognize that it was my husband until he screamed, *"Bitch!! You think I am a fuckin' fool don't you! I swear to God I'll kill you bitch!"*

I opened my eyes for a spilt second to see his face and when I did, all I saw was a demonic figure that was pure black with blood-shot red eyes and foam, like from an angry dog, coming from his mouth. His breathing was like a growl and there was a foul odor in the room; a stench that I cannot describe. Then another hard strike to the left side of my head while I lay curled up in the fetal position to protect myself the best way that I knew how. I figured that if I did not move to avoid his assault, and if I stopped screaming, the attack would stop. My screams did not stop. I could not stop them, nor could I control the volume because my head felt like it was about to explode from what felt like a hammer being used to hit me repeatedly. I heard him say, *"Motherfucker, I'll beat you to a fuckin' pulp and your own fuckin' family will not recognize your ass. Bitch, I promise I'll kill you today."*

When I heard those words, immediately I thought about Jaidan. There was something that came over me. There was no way I was dying and leaving my baby. And I surely could not die this way. I said within myself, after what seemed like an eternity, "GOD save me" …. Jaidan began to cry.

He had me cornered on the floor between the wall that separated my living room from my bedroom and the front door, and he was bent over me just beating me, pounding on me, and I could not crawl away. I tried. I had absolutely no energy and I was terrified.

However, Jaidan's cries turned to screams and it caught his attention. Her ear-piercing screaming, it seemed, caused him to stop hitting me, but he did not stop screaming at me and telling me that he was going to kill me. He kept saying to me that I made him do it. He said multiple times, *"Bitch! Look what you made me do. You did this Bitch. I hope you're fuckin' happy. You are a stupid bitch! I should've left your motherfuckin' stupid ass in the Strip Club where I found your dumb ass. Fuckin' slut! That's what you are bitch. A fuckin' ho. Bitch I'll kill your ass."*

He went into the master bedroom, grabbed Jai from her crib and left. I begged him, with what little voice that I had left from my own screaming and crying; I pleaded for him not to take my baby. I got up as quickly as I could, only to keep stumbling to the floor because my head was hurting so badly that I honestly couldn't see clearly, nor could I keep my balance. Once I heard his truck leaving the driveway, I mustered up the strength to get the house phone from the kitchen counter. He had my cell phone with him. I knew he did because he used it to slap me across my face with it when he said to me, *"You did this Bitch!*

I made my way into my bedroom, locked the door behind me and went into my master bath and locked the door there also. I was able to call 911. When the operator answered my call and asked me to state my emergency, the only thing I had the strength to say is, *"He is coming back to kill me. Please hurry"*. I was physically shaking, filled with terror, and I could hardly speak. My voice was at a minimum and extremely hoarse.

I believe that I kept losing consciousness because I felt so dizzy that I wanted to vomit and then the room would suddenly go black. I do remember the 911 operator saying to me, *"Do Not Hang Up! I am sending help"*.

I do not know how long it took the Halifax County Sheriff's office to respond. I have no recollection of the time. I do though, remember crawling into my garden bathtub where there was a window. From there, because the tub was deep, I could hide, but I could also hear cars or his truck when he returned because my driveway was on that side of my home. I had also locked both my bedroom door and bathroom door which would buy me more time if he got there before help had come. The doors could not be opened from the outside of the rooms. He would have to find a tool or kick them down.

It was not until the officers showed up to my home that I even knew what made him attack me like he did. I did remember him slapping me in the face with my cellphone and shoving it in my face.

He pulled out my cell phone again. He told one of the officers that he had evidence that I was cheating on him with a Highway Patrol Officer, and he knew him personally and was going to pursue legally to have him fired. LIES!! He was such a LIAR!! He showed them my phone which had a multi-media message of a framed graduation photo that read, "Good morning, Beautiful". It was a multimedia post of my friend in uniform when he graduated, many years prior, from HP Training School!! Oh, the stories that my husband created and exaggerated. The endless lies that he manipulated everyone with concerning a relationship that never existed. This man clearly was deranged. I did not realize that any person could be demonically possessed until I married a demon in the flesh.

What I remember next was a deputy taking photos of my injuries and sending me to get medical attention and then to the Courthouse to stand before the judge to have an ex-parte order drawn up for the protection of myself and Jaidan. I was forced to leave my home, with my baby girl, and find temporary safe shelter for the both of us.

When he had to show up before the judge, after nearly taking my life, he did the whole fake cry with the lies, that he was "SO AFRAID" of losing his family!!! Narcissism at its FINEST!! This man hated my guts and he proved it to me. He hired a lawyer to keep him from being convicted of domestic violence abuse. He played the victim and used the- *"he is supposed to uphold the law"* line against my friend, time after time. My husband presented himself as if, he had done no wrong in attempting to murder me and declaring that he would. He was so convinced of his own lies that he told them with pride and arrogance. It's as if his mind was reprobate. I was sick to my stomach.

As he had threatened, he went after the gentleman, to his superiors, with false accusations, demanding to have an internal investigation done that led nowhere. His story was filled with lies and others could clearly see through them. He only did this to "cover" himself and his hidden agenda.

See, while I had to leave my home for 30 days to find safe shelter for my daughter and myself, my husband was out hiring an attorney, while at the same time gathering information on where the HP officer lived and stalking my every move. He would, knowing that he was not supposed to be near me, show up in the parking lot of my job with his gun laying on the dashboard where I could see it. PURE EVIL!! He only hired the attorney and gave the sob stories filled with lies to make himself seem like the victim! He was always the victim. I was terrified to stay away from him and even more terrified to go back.

He began having his best friend, at the time, meet me places to pick up our daughter so that he could see her. He used her as a pawn to get me and his "family" back. Jaidan and I, eventually, after 4 months of living in a friend's house, went back home.

I was not even back at my home and settled in for a good two months when someone showed up to my home around 2 o'clock in the morning blowing the car horn, screaming, and crying in the driveway next to my bedroom window. I jumped up frantically, and calmed my goddaughter and Jaidan after they too were awakened and scared because of all the ruckus. I then put my robe on and stepped outside on the front porch to see what all the commotion was. It was her, my husband's side chick. Drunk and belligerent. The way she was most every weekend that she was out partying and sneaking out with someone's husband.

She was hanging out of the back passenger window of the car, screaming at the tops of her lungs that she had to tell me how long she had been with my husband, how they were in love and that he was going to put me out of my home, and she and her boys were moving in.

I asked her to leave a few times and when she didn't take heed, I then demanded that she- *"get the fuck off my lawn"*. I did not want to hear anything that she had to say. I'm yelling at her and she's yelling at me and blowing the car horn and her two friends in the car are cheering her on and adding fuel to the fire. I started screaming for my husband to get her off my lawn. I told him that if she were not off my lawn by the time I got my gun from the top of the refrigerator, she would lay where she stood. I walked back in my house and heard the cries of my baby, the look of terror in my goddaughter's eyes and felt the rage that continued to build within me...

When I tell you that I could be somebody's cellmate...? Please believe me! Remember when I told you earlier my words to her were, *"This shit just got really personal"*; well, this was the day that "shit" got personal. I don't know if you remember a show that used to come on the Oxygen channel called *Snapped*. It was about women, most of them having a history of being physically abused domestically, who had committed murder because, well, one day when it became too much they just *snapped*. Well, on October 29, 2006, at approximately 2:30am,

I grabbed the loaded 9mm Glock from the top of my refrigerator and proceeded out of my front door, I screamed one last time, *"GET THE FUCK OFF MY LAWN"*, then I raised the gun aimed straight at her face. Her friends started screaming for her to get in the car. Too late now. Don't try to talk her down when you were cheering her on just two minutes ago. My ex screamed, *"TASHA! THINK ABOUT JAI!"* He then tackled me to the ground and was able to get the gun from me. I fought with him to get him off me. I got myself off the ground after a few minutes of tussling with him. I then went back in the house to get both my girls and was able to finally calm them by getting them both back in my bed. They could not sleep, but they were better. My babies were so scared.

I had gotten snacks for them and turned-on cartoons. I tucked them in and made sure they were good. Jai was not quite two years old, and my goddaughter was ten years old. I got dressed, kissed them both and told my goddaughter that I would be back. He was sitting on the sofa just outside of my bedroom, so when I walked out, he asked where I was going. I told him that I was going to take a warrant out against her for trespassing. She had a history of doing this crazy mess with other women concerning their husbands. But I was not allowing her to play these petty games with me and for her to think that once the dust settled that she would do this again. I had the options of dragging her and going to jail afterwards or filing charges against her for trespassing and allowing the courts to make an example of her. I chose the option with no consequences to myself. Now, in no stretch of the imagination was I a "bad tail" or someone that even came across as "bad" in the way of fighting; however, I was absolutely not the one that you wanted to cross either. Funny, how I allowed myself to be beat up physically and torn down mentally by my husband but never allowed anyone else to bully me. By this time though, I was no longer afraid of him.

I had made up my mind that if he ever put his hands on me, at all, in any aggressive manner, I would put holes in him. This is the -In JESUS' Name Truth! At this point, I hated this man with every fiber of my being. Even being around him made me so sick and disgusted. The smell of him made my stomach turn. The sound of his voice made my skin crawl. I hated this man so much so that I hated to breathe the same air that he breathed. This hatred for him began to take root in my heart so deep that I had begun contemplating killing him. I mean literally, killing him DEAD!

I had sat on my sofa many, and I mean many times where I could see directly into the mudroom where the backdoor entrance was. I would sit there for hours on end meditating on just how I would be able to have a clear shot of his head from that position. I had recounted and replayed the exact scenario from beginning to end, including the insanity plea in court and how my daughter and I would live happily ever after.

This went on for months in my mind. I would imagine him walking in through the backdoor, me raising the gun and with one single shot, blowing his brains out. I could visualize seeing his blood splattered all over the walls and hearing him gasping for air as I stood over him watching him, watch me, as he took his last breath. Then I would end up dialing 911 as a domestic call and claim having to defend myself against him attacking me again. I would finally have vengeance and he could no longer play the victim. Finally, I would have made him pay for all that he had ever done to me, and he would die with the regret of every foul word that he had ever spoken to me and all the names that he had ever called me. He would never be able to torture me again.

However, when I had gotten to the place in my mind where I could visualize his dead bloody body and it did not even cause my conscious to be bothered in the least bit, I knew I had to get away from him or I was capable of no longer "meditating" his murder, I could possibly murder this man without hesitation. The hate that I had for him had become extremely dangerous and this made me extremely afraid for his life and mine.

My own thoughts terrified me. I was haunted by the movie-like horror images that had begun to plague my mind constantly. I knew that our marriage was over, but even more than that, I desperately had to get away from this man. I had to save myself and gain my freedom from him. I do not agree with, nor have I ever, the taking of anyone's life. However, I can honestly say that I do understand how one may end up in that exact place. The place where- Enough is ENOUGH!

Chapter 17:
Forgiveness

Abused, hated, and rejected by my first love, my mother. Rejected and abandoned by the first man in my life, my father. The reason why I hated "white" men and the smell of Old Spice Cologne and why I cringe and must turn the television when an Old Spice Cologne commercial plays, still to this day, is because I was sexually molested by my mom's white boyfriend, and that was the fragrance that he wore. I had lesbian encounters because I felt safe with girls and felt like we shared some of the same insecurities. I was looking for love in all the wrong places. My virginity was taken from me at the age of 17 and it felt like death to me. I had a five-year long affair with a married man and there were a few more during that span of time. I was the epitome of a fantasy or "trophy" girl. I would go from the Dance Hall to the Strip Clubs. I lived seven and a half years on the road as a "featured dancer". I was in the strip clubs, getting high, getting paid and selling my body for the attention. I thought meeting my ex equated to being in love because I finally had a commitment. Instead, I found myself entrapped by jealousy, control, manipulation, abuse, and violence; mentally, emotionally, physically and spiritually. Then the devastation of the diagnosis of 'Unexplainable Infertility' that led to having five surgeries in the hopes of getting pregnant and the reality of three babies in Heaven. (Two during fertility treatments in 2003).

Love: All the things that I thought love was! I never knew love. I knew that there were people that cared about me; NOT LOVE!

Orville, My Father….NO!
Debra, My Mother…NO!

…Funny thing is the one and main thing that I wanted and sought after, and even that I gave, is the one thing that I never knew. However, it was "somehow" IN me. Through all the hell and mistreatment, rejection, abandonment, deaths, hatred, bashing, shame, guilt, lies, dishonesty, confusion, pain, heartache, hurt, condemnation, self-hatred, abuse, betrayal, and well, I could go on and on… There was something deep down within me that made me kind, gentle, compassionate, caring and nurturing. Even toward those that mistreated and mishandled me.

"Pillar to Post", my grandmother's word. I have heard those words concerning my life since I was a girl of my youth. Maybe as young as seven or so. She would often say, even well into my adult life, *"Child, you have been thrown from pillar to post your whole life"*. I am 45, and I still hear the continuation of that sentence, …*"just like little stray kittens"*. Sad but true. Wherever I could stay and for however long someone was willing to "keep" me. Black garbage bags were my option for luggage.

Whenever I had to "pack up", it was always in black garbage bags that all of my belongings were kept.

From NC to VA to NC to VA to NC…. And you wonder why I have issues???!!!???? And you must ponder and ask yourself why I have trust issues?

There's more…

Chapter 18:
Forgiveness: Seeking Support

In the year of 2006, I was still attending the Kingdom Hall of Jehovah's Witnesses. I had gone to the elders of the congregation to seek their help concerning the volatile state of my marriage. I knew, according to the Scriptures, that I was supposed to go to the elders. It was also the protocol of the Governing Body to make family matters known, especially those that would have an effect on attendance and ministry. I made a few phone calls to some of the brothers that were elders in the Kingdom Hall that I attended and asked them to meet with me. I shared with each of them the events that transpired after my husband's brutal attack on me that could have costed my life. I shared this on every call with every person that I had to speak with. I can only assume that they conversed amongst themselves about the information that I had given them and came up with a solution. I waited a couple of days to hear back from our Presiding Overseer with a time to meet with him and the elders. Once I received that call, I could hardly breathe from the response. *"Sister Hunter, we have had time to present this information to the Governing Body and have been advised against having a meeting with you. We do not get involved in marital issues. Those things should only be worked out between a husband and wife. However, we have been given instruction to interview you, since your husband is not a Jehovah's Witness, as to whether you should remain active or even in the congregation"*. There were other words spoken, I am sure of it, I just did not hear them. I was so hurt. I was confused. I hung up the phone and sat down on the dining room floor in tears and with my mouth left wide open. What had just happened to me? What did he say? I was a Baptized WITNESS! I was ACTIVE in all my duties as a WITNESS! I was in shock to say the least and even more, once again, left to fend for myself; by myself. REJECTED!! I felt like I walked around with that word tattooed on my forehead.

Now let me take you back six years prior. July 14, 2000, Richmond Coliseum, where the 2000 Convention "Doers of The Word" was held, around 11:30am and I was in anticipation. This was "The DAY". I had prepared for this day as a very young child. In September of 1998, after not attending meetings since 1993, I had returned to the Kingdom Hall, and I was serving faithfully in the ministry. I was doing my best to cross every "t" and dot every "i". I had to prove myself to the elders of the Congregation that I was worthy to be baptized. I was faithful, every week, in my home Bible Study and even chaperoned when going out in Field Service. I was recording hours even with having a part-time job and attending Community College. I also had to let the elders of the congregation and the sisters that were leading my home studies know that I was preparing for marriage, because I did not want anything to hinder my walk. I was doing everything by the book to "show yourself approved". I was married in April of 1999, so because I was married now, I could lead in the Field Ministry. I was faithful. I was excited and very disciplined. I made every meeting, every Special Talk, every Memorial celebration, and every

Convention for the full three days. I saved my vacation time to be able to attend.

I was so excited to receive the approval of the Governing Body. I was asked to stand at the Kingdom Hall when the announcement and the Letter was read in front of the entire Congregation. I wept. I could hardly control my emotions. I had been accepted! I could be Baptized! My diligent work and dedication were enough. I had proven myself worthy of the honor to be called "Sister" and take part in water baptism. I could hardly wait to get in my car and call my G'ma. As soon as she answered, I screamed out with JOY!! I cried, she cried, we cried more and praised Jehovah! I could not thank Him enough for allowing the Governing Body to make such a decision that would forever change my life. I was accepted!! We finally calmed down and G'ma told me how happy she was for me. As our conversation was coming to close, I asked her if she would contact my Uncle Clarence and Aunt Linda to tell them the good news. G'ma replied that she would be grateful to share the news!

"Uncle" Clarence, as I always called him, though he was my biological distant relative, was at least 40 years my senior. He was a very gentle and kind man. I never heard him speak ill, nor had I ever heard him raise his voice. I had remembered him since I was a little bitty girl all the way up through my teenage years. Even when I was in the world, he would call my G'ma to ask of my well-being. When I was with my G'ma, between the ages of seven to maybe twelve or thirteen, he and his wife, Aunt Linda, would allow me to spend time with them. I loved it too because they both loved to cook, and so did I. They did not have children together, though Uncle Clarence had children from his previous marriage. Because he was family, he knew of my upbringing and my struggles. I was hoping that he would come to Richmond for my baptism. I somehow always felt like he "really" prayed for me when he said that he did. I felt that he "genuinely" loved me when he said he did. I was hoping and praying that he would be there.

The day came. It was the day of my baptism. All the chosen ones are asked to rise from our seats. There is a beautiful oath that we must repeat in answer to the questions of our dedication. It is our vow of our life's dedication to Jehovah and to the faithful spreading of the "Good News". The tears are streaming down my face, and I am sobbing so loudly that I can hear my echo in the atmosphere. Everyone else is silent, as is the custom. Only the voices of those that are being baptized are heard throughout the entire Coliseum that holds thousands of Witnesses. There was a "feeling" that came over me as I was making my outward confession of my faith. I could not explain what was happening inside of me and causing me to have this outpour. I gathered my backpack to make my way to the restroom to change into my water clothes and then proceeded to the baptismal pool. With poor health, but overwhelming joy that streamed from his eyes, as I came down the last set of stairs and into the open floor and walked towards the area for the ladies' restrooms, Uncle Clarence was there with his camera in hand. I ran towards him and wrapped my arms tightly around his neck! We both held one another in that embrace as if time had stopped just for the both of us. He whispered to me, "Jehovah is so pleased". I felt like I had seen an Angel of the LORD. He captured every moment of my baptism. Once I had changed out of my wet clothes, and hurried to get back into my dress clothing, I walked out hastily, anticipating that he was still there. He was gone. I looked around for him almost in a panic. I asked my G'ma where he had gone. She said, *"Your Uncle told me to tell you that he was not able to stay. He was not feeling well, but he was not going to miss this moment for anything in the world. He says, thank you for wanting him to be here and he will mail all the photos to you once they are developed. He also said to tell you that he loves you and he is so happy that this day came for you, and he was hoping that he would live to see it."*

I received the envelope in the mail, postage marked August 3, 2000. The letter inside was written and dated August 2, 2000.

"Dear Tasha,

Linda and I thank you so much for your card. It was nice of you to write. As you know, we think quite a lot of you. We always have. I had always hoped that you would find the keys to life before you got hurt too much. So, your baptism was sheer joy for me. It is my sincere wish that you continue to serve our great God Jehovah and always rely on Him despite anything that ever happens to you. Please share the photos with your Grandmother. If you need any of the negatives just let me know. I am so happy for you!

Love, Bro Hall"

I have this letter still in my keepsake box. He even numbered the photos in the order in which they were taken. I take it out and read it often as a gentle reminder not only of the love and compassion shown towards me from Uncle Clarence, but more for the Love of Jehovah demonstrated through him for me. It may not seem deep and overflowing with words of compassion to others, however for me, it is filled to the overflow with love. I feel the Heart of Abba every time I read it and look at the pictures of my baptism.

Chapter 19:
Forgiveness: *"Help Me!"*

In 2008 I am praying for "deliverance and restoration" daily. I honestly have no idea what these two words even mean. I know that I have read throughout Scripture that Jehovah is my Deliverer and that He Restores. That is all that I know.

Ever since I returned home in October of 2006, there had been no more physical violence and abuse. The mental and emotional abuse remained, and the residue of "what was" still haunted me. I never put anything past anyone that would try to take my life with his bare hands.

Every day on my way to work I would turn off the radio if it were on. I would ride in silence, even at times placing my cell phone on silent. I would, in my mind, pray and ask GOD for deliverance and restoration.

The entire thirty-minute one-way drive was this way. It was the same on the way home. I would tell GOD that this was not a marriage and if I had to stay with this man, I was scared that the day would come that either he would kill me, or I would kill him. I already knew what he was capable of and not just because of the last time. This man, with our daughter in the back seat of his vehicle, chased me southbound on

Interstate 95, at speeds of over 90 miles per hour, and attempted to run me off the highway. He was swerving in and out of traffic to get close to me to force me to wreck. I drove faster to get away from him, not realizing at the time, that I was endangering my daughter's life by fleeing. I thought maybe, just maybe, he would have enough sense to stop. This lasted for nearly an hour. From Enfield, North Carolina to just past the outskirts of Fayetteville, North Carolina, he chased me.

There was an elderly couple driving a white Toyota Camry with Florida tags that noticed. I could see them moving closer to my car to get beside me. I was crying and screaming in my car for him to stop. The couple, because traffic began to slow down due to some congestion, got beside me in the left lane and I looked over at them and just motioned my lips and said, *"Help Me"*.

The gentleman, driving, motioned for me to get in the lane front of them. The woman called for emergency help and the North Carolina Highway Patrol was on the next ramp with lights. My husband kept passing and then texted me, *"Your guardian angels saved you today"*. All I could do was cry and thank God. I ended up staying at a hotel that night in Lumberton. So, when I tell you that this man could kill me, I know he could do it in more ways than one. He was pure evil.

September 15, 2010...

After working nearly twelve hours, I came home to find my husband there with a friend from Georgia. He and the friend had planned to go to Rocky Mount to get food once I got home. They didn't leave until I arrived home because Jaidan was with them, and it was already after 9'oclock at night. It was her bedtime, and I was exhausted from the long day at Verizon Wireless. The day of standing on my feet in five and a half inch heels was a lot. I was ready to wind down, shower, and get in bed. My husband shouted from the kitchen that they would be back in a while, and he locked the door behind him and left. I cuddled and loved on Jai for a bit and then laid across the bed with her for about ten minutes. I then pulled back the covers and got Jai in the bed with cartoons on the television so she could relax and be entertained while I showered. I knew she would fall asleep by the time I was done in the shower.

I went to the bathroom at the end of my hallway to start the water. The temperature was perfect, so I got in and pulled the shower curtain. I may have been in the shower for five minutes when I thought I heard knocking. I pulled the shower curtain back and opened the bathroom door a little and listened to see if I did hear something. As soon as I closed the door, I heard that sound again. I cracked the door open and kept saying, *"Hold on. I'm Coming"*. I thought maybe my husband had forgotten something and had the set of keys with just the truck key on it. Before I could get my towel wrapped good, the knocking turned to banging. I was angry now because I thought he was being funny or in a mood. So, once I got to the back door, I quickly opened it. To my utter shock, there were three men standing along my stairs and all three had flashlights! Immediately, my heart fell to the floor. I began to panic. The man closest to me asked me if I knew, and he mentioned my husband's name, and I said, *"Yes Sir"*. I started to cry because I could tell that they were cops and I thought that my husband had been in an accident, and they had found his driver's license. I did not know what to say and I had forgotten for a second that I was standing wrapped in my bath towel. I apologized and told the officer that I would have to put my clothes on. I was completely dazed and confused. I felt as if I was dreaming. Was this really happening? I can recall walking into my bedroom, seeing Jai laying on the bed asleep, and then standing in my closet, just standing there as if I had forgotten that I needed clothes to dress.

After getting dressed, I walked out of my bedroom and when I turned the corner back into my kitchen, there were officers standing there, and many whose faces I clearly recognized. I began to cry harder. I still did not know what was happening. One of the officers spoke up and told me his name and that he was from the SBI and had a warrant to search my home. He began to read the explanation of the warrant and I felt as if the wind had been kicked from my chest. I just stared at the paper, with tears soaking the pages. I could not grasp it. I remember looking at the faces of the officers that I knew, and they were looking at me in what appeared to be pure shock.

The lead officer of the SBI asked me who else lived in my home, who was presently in the house, and if I had somewhere "SAFE" for me and my daughter to go. My mind was spinning. I was in, what seemed to be, a living nightmare. I could not gather my thoughts. A search warrant? Are you sure? How did this happen? Why do I need a "safe place"? Are we, my daughter and I, in danger? Where is he? Can I get clothes for me and my baby? How long will I have to leave? What is going to happen to my home? Where do I go? I have nowhere to go!

I honestly cannot begin to tell you all the questions and fears that were flooding my thoughts. I had no comprehension of what was happening right before my very eyes. I felt I was in a scene of a suspense movie. Once I was able to slow my thoughts, the same officer told me that my husband had already been taken into custody and was outside in a patrol car. He stated that I could speak to him if I wanted to. I walked out of my back door and down the stairs to the car that I was directed to.

The blue lights from the police cars appeared to light up my entire property of nearly six acres in the pitch-black dark. There appeared to be a sea of police cars that covered my lawn. I was shaking like I was freezing and honestly in shock. He was in the backseat; another officer opened the back door where he sat. He did not say a word to me. He just looked at me. I wanted to scream at him, punch him in the face, and rescue him all at the same time. My emotions were like a runaway train going one hundred miles per hour downhill and gaining momentum. I stood there waiting, expecting "something", anything… What I got was absolutely nothing.

Chapter 20:
Shattered

Overnight I became a "single mom". I was already doing most things for Jai on my own, however, at least her dad was there. He may not have been a good husband or a good dad, but she loved him. He was good to her when everything was good between us. I do know that she had fun with him. He taught her to ride a 250 Honda Recon when she was not quite four years old. I would be so scared; however, I was filled with joy for her bravery at such a young age. There was no fear in her at all. I did my best to make sure that she was always loved and protected. So, the night of September 15, 2010, was the beginning of events that I do not believe I could have ever prepared for. I know that I prayed for deliverance and restoration, however, I could have never imagined this. I could have never imagined that what I prayed for would be answered in this way. I could have never imagined lying to my baby about the whereabouts of her daddy. I told the same lie, day after day, doing everything within my power to protect her sweet little heart and to stop her midnight cries that went on for months. The heart cries that filled my bedroom and her sweet tears soaked my chest because she just wanted to see her daddy and could never understand why she could not. I had been called many things during this time by him and his family, names unimaginable. Yet, no one was there when I had to pick my baby up and hold her for what seemed like days and nights because her little heart was broken. The abandonment even from his family was overwhelming. I understood that they never cared anything at all for me, but to abandon the baby was just hateful.

In the span of the next three years, my ex-husband was sentenced to seven and a half years in Federal prison, I was laid off from my job, my cars were repossessed, my home was foreclosed on, I miscarried baby number three and delivered the baby in my hands on the toilet, attempted suicide, and Jai and I were homeless. I was diagnosed with having manic depression, hospitalized due to anxiety, and clinically diagnosed with Post Traumatic Stress Disorder (PTSD).

How did I end up in this place?

Chapter 21:
Safe Haven

There have only been three men in my life that I have ever felt safe around and DJ is one of them. I know that I am really about to mess some of you up and you might take this book outside and burn it. I warned you from the very beginning that this is not for the weak and faint of heart, this is my story and I get to tell it truthfully. I have been forgiven and I have also prayed for all those that I have hurt. As you read in previous chapters, I am no saint and I have reaped consequences. I thank Abba Father for His Mercy and His Grace; however, I have still been whopped by my choices.

Back to DJ. DJ was married into the same family that I was. Our exes are siblings. I know...I know. I can promise you that he was not on my radar nor ANY BODY that I was even close to being romantically interested in. I thought to myself, if he married into this family, and as crazy as she is, something has got to be wrong with him. I promise you on everything, I told my biological sister that he must have been mentally challenged to marry into this family and to marry a woman that plays with Ouija boards and talks to demons and has full blown conversations with spirits that she named after her brother, my husband! This was a whole different kind of crazy and demonic possession. I am in no way making light of this because demons are real, and I believe it is a generational curse. Listen, I pray that she has repented and received Salvation in Jesus Christ, been delivered, and set completely free. DJ was my friend. When the entire family turned their backs on me and Jaidan, he became a good friend. He had been in the family long enough to see from the outside, the turmoil in my marriage. He understood what Jaidan was going through with her daddy being in prison and would bring snacks for her and ride with her and my nephews on the four-wheeler. She had so much fun with him, and to be honest, after all the hell that I was still processing through, he was like a breath of fresh air. Not so much for me, but for my sweet girl.

Fast forward to April 2012, I was really starting to see DJ in another light. It had taken me by surprise, because I had been so consumed with trying to maintain a home with one income that did not compare to what was before my husband went to prison. In addition, my job was talking about restructuring the workplace to no longer have my position in the stores. MY GOD!!! Do things EVER get better for me? So, while I was doing everything possible just to keep my head above water to breathe, I have the audacity to be drawn to this man. I remember the day it happened like it was this afternoon, the day that I knew I was in love with DJ. He had come over and was in my back yard with the children. They were wanting to ride the four-wheeler, but it needed gas. So, one of my nephews went over to DJ's house and asked if he would get gas for them to ride. Of course, he did. Once he got back from the store, I heard the children laughing and being loud in the back yard, so looking out of the kitchen window, I could see them running around him and the four-wheeler in pure excitement as if they had never ridden before! Pure joy that warmed my heart.

I was washing dishes and cleaning my home, since I had the weekend off. It was Saturday morning, about 70 degrees, and I had all the windows raised to let in the fresh air. I had music playing while cleaning and was simply happy. I must be honest, I thought for a second, "This is how I imagine marriage and family. My husband outside with the children playing while I am cleaning and making dinner". I was just in a great mood. So, as I was standing at the kitchen sink, I looked up and she was walking across my back yard to speak to DJ. My heart dropped to my feet and immediately I felt like vomiting… I was in love with her man. NO! This was not happening! No Way!! Was I freaking crazy? I needed to check myself quick! But the reality was, that I was very much so in love with him. I walked to my bedroom and sat on the edge of my bed. I heard the back door open and within a minute he was standing in the doorway to my bedroom. He did not speak right away, because I honestly knew that he knew what I was feeling because he was feeling the same way. He walked over to me and lifted my face towards him with his finger under my chin and he said to me, "What's wrong". My face was soaked with tears, and I just shook my head from side to side as to say, "nothing". But he knew. He kissed me on my forehead and walked away with his head hung down. That evening he texted me and asked if he could come over. I said, "*Sure.*"

We ended up having an extremely lust-filled, passionate sex life, a full-blown affair, that led me to getting pregnant. Now mind you, I had NEVER gotten pregnant naturally! EVER! I did not know that I was pregnant because I never believed that I would get pregnant naturally. I was so stressed out! June 9, 2012, I delivered our 12-week-old baby in my hands in the most painful way imaginable. I awoke with the worst menstrual cramps just before 6am. It felt as if someone had their hand inside of me with a pair of vice grips and had clamped down on my cervix and uterus and began to rip them from my body. I could feel what literally felt like tearing. I have had procedures to scrape my uterus after a miscarriage and this was far worse than that. DJ was still married and living with his wife at this time. He was working though this morning and I was at home alone with Jaidan. I went to the bathroom at the end of the hallway because Jaidan was sleeping in my bed, and I was crying because I was in so much pain. I could hardly stand to walk. I ran water in the bath to get in to soak hoping that the hot water would help the cramps to stop, or at least give me some relief. After soaking in the tub for about twenty minutes, I started to bleed. So, I got out of the tub and sat on the toilet. I could feel, what seemed to me, to be a big blood clot passing. I had never passed blood clots this big where I could feel this type of sensation. It never crossed my mind that is could be anything else! I wrapped my hand with tissue and said within myself, 'I am going to catch this blood-clot, because I have never passed anything like this'. I could feel it inching down and I was starting to panic and cry harder because the pain was not easing up. The pain and sensations intensified. This had to go on record as the most painful period ever. I braced myself because I could feel it getting closer to my vaginal opening, and once I gave a little push to help it come out, it was not a clot at all! I recognized it right away! I knew it was a baby. I could see baby's eyes, tiny arms, the rib cage, and tiny fingers. The bottom half of baby was covered with "matter". I called DJ and when he did not answer I sent him a photo of baby! I held baby for maybe three hours. I was so afraid to put my baby down. DJ called me as soon as he could and he, I could tell, was upset. Neither of us knew. He said later that he thought maybe I was pregnant because he had been getting sick at work and he never was sick on the stomach. I made an appointment with my Ob/Gyn to bring baby in and to have a checkup. Things started to turn in the relationship that DJ and I were building. To this day, I think that he blames me for the miscarriage. Why? Because months later, he asked me why I did not go and get checked out when my period kept being spotty the first two months. I honestly, put it off as stress. Pregnancy never crossed my mind.

After losing baby, one month later, July 15, 2012, I lost my job. Certainly things cannot get any worse. Yet by the time February 2013 had come, the bank had started the foreclosure process on my home. My cars had already been repossessed, and the only vehicle that I had was my husband's. My Jaidan and I were facing being homeless.

"Look at you! You are no better than her daddy! You cannot provide for yourself, nor can you even provide for her. Where are you going to live? How are you going to take care of Jaidan? You are nothing but a failure! She is better off without you! You cannot take care of her. You should just end it! After all, what do you have left? No cars, you pawned all your jewelry, and now you do not even

have a home to put her in. Failure is what you are. She deserves better that you."
These were the lies that I listened to driving to get Jaidan from school and all the way back home. The enemy said everything to convince me that I should just pack up all Jaidan's clothes, call my Aunt Ginny and tell her to come and get Jaidan. Then once she had gotten her, I should "end it". Besides, Jaidan deserved so much more than a parent in prison and the one left to care for her and protect her had lost everything including her home. "Don't kill yourself while she's here", he said. "Wait until she is gone. You wouldn't want her to find your body". When I tell you, Satan is so cunning that he will tell you how to murder yourself and clean up the crime scene as if he cares for you! I must admit, in my state of mind, I was convinced. At least for a moment.

I remember arriving in the car line to get Jai and the enemy just kept talking. I was doing everything in my power to stop the tears from streaming down my face. I was devastated and even more once my baby got into the vehicle and asked me if I could get her a $5 pizza... I choked up so bad, having to tell my baby that I did not even have five dollars to get her a personal pizza. Five Dollars! All that I had was a twenty-dollar bill and that was gas to get her to and from school, from Enfield to Rocky Mount daily. By this time, in my mind, the enemy no longer had to convince me; I was in total agreement. She does deserve better, and I am a failure. Her dad and I had failed her. She never asked for this life! I did not deserve her either. Abba Father answered my prayers, and this is how I repay Him? By losing my job, losing my home, sleeping with another married woman's husband, and getting pregnant by him? Yes! I deserve to die today! I cried all the way home. As soon as I got home, I told Jaidan to watch tv and I went straight into my bedroom. I closed the door behind me and walked into my master bathroom to look myself in the mirror. I could not believe the disgust that I saw when I looked at myself. I do not remember if I spoke words or stood in silence, nor for how long. What I do remember is reaching under the mattress on my side of the bed and pulling out the loaded gun.

"What are you doing? Wait! Call Aunt Ginny! Do not let Jaidan find you like this. She will only blame herself". 'SHUT UP! "If you're going to do it, put the gun under your pillow and lay your head right where you can feel the barrel. It will be over before you know it. You won't feel a thing."

So, I fixed my pillow at the foot of my bed. I placed the gun in my left hand, although I am right-handed, and I cradled the handle of the gun against my fingers and placed my thumb on the trigger. I was on my knees to make sure that I adjusted myself properly, before lying flat on my stomach. I looked at the time on the alarm clock that was on my nightside table, and it was 4:43 pm. I turned my head towards the right, facing my closet, so that the bullet would travel through the left side of my head. I began to shake so much that my body started to shiver. I could no longer hold the gun steady. My crying had turned to hyperventilation and panic until I felt that I was no longer in control of my own body nor my thoughts. I was still on my knees and terror had completely gripped me as I laid my head on the pillow.

I could feel the gun pressed against my temple, and the only words that came from my mouth in a whisper..." Father, Help me."

When I awoke, I opened my eyes in panic and immediately tears streamed down my face. I looked at the time and it was 5:39am. My sweet Jaidan was laying on the same pillow with me and she had gotten her Dora the Explorer blanket and covered both our bodies with it. I kissed her precious face as she was sleeping so peacefully, and I whispered to her, "Mommy is sorry. I will never leave you." I got up from my bed and went into my living room, fell on my face and I begged God to forgive me, and I could not thank Him enough for saving me by putting me to sleep. I begged Him to forgive me for not feeding my baby and not bathing her or caring for her that entire day.

I must be honest with you, before this happened to me, I was quick to say, "how could anything be so bad that someone would take their own life?" I promise you on everything, I NEVER have had that thought again. Now I know that because of the Calling that is on my life, I must be equipped with the compassion of Christ to reach those that may be suicidal or living with the stigma of suicidal thoughts. Did God place that on me? Absolutely not, however, He did allow it to happen for His Glory. "What the enemy meant for evil (to kill me), GOD turned it for His Good."

The year 2013 was quite the year of tests and attacks. When I tell you that Satan pulled out every weapon that he could pull against me to take me out, mentally, physically and spiritually, I am not joking. After the suicide attempt did not work, foreclosure of my home and sleeping on my sister's couch, being labeled 'homeless' and a "displaced US Citizen, did not work, I guess he said to himself, "Let me try one more attempt." And, well, that is exactly what he did.

June of 2013, I began working again and I was able to move into a beautiful new rental. DJ moved in with me and Jaidan. A few months after we were all living in our new "happily ever after", I sensed a change in DJ. He was demonstrating behaviors that were awfully familiar to me; behaviors like when I was either cheating or being cheated on. I will not go into all the details, just know this... Some things you just "know". And I was spot on. I began to warn him about the dreams that I was having and even what the Holy Spirit was revealing to me outside of the dreams. Of course, I was deemed crazy! Until it all came to the light...

Chapter 22:
He *Was* My Safe Haven Until
He Wasn't!

December 1, 2013, I found out that DJ had been having an affair with a young woman and not just a sneak around creepin' type of mess, I mean this was like him having two separate families. When it all came to the light and it always does, DJ and this young woman were planning to get pregnant. So, not just movie and dinner mess, I mean pictures of ovulation kits and scheduling when they would meet at the hotel or her place to have sex to go half on a baby! I am in no way sharing this traumatic time in our lives to bash my husband, nor to air our dirty laundry, however, I am writing this for the sake of sharing with you, that this needed to happen. Crazy right? I know. I mean it. This was necessary for ME!

For years, I had put DJ up on a pedestal and made him my god. He was my absolute EVERYTHING! And I do mean EVERY-THING! I worshiped the ground that this man walked on. There was nothing and no part of me that was off limits to him, even though currently he was still someone else's husband living with me. Listen, I know I was wrong and in no way am I justifying any of this, nor will I ever. I remember when this happened, how he broke me like no man had ever broken me. I had never loved any other man the way that I loved DJ. I gave up everything for him and had dedicated myself completely to him. I remember vividly, unfortunately, the night that I saw her photo on his phone and I picked the phone up off the bedroom floor and the phone, for the first time, did not have the lock code on it; Holy Spirit will bypass your security code! He was in the shower, and I walked into the laundry room on the other end of the house, and I opened the message thread. Just know this, when "Trouble" knocks on your door one of two things will happen. Either all the "Jesus" that you talk about and have been filling yourself with will show up, or all that "Hell" that you have not been delivered from will. You have only got a 50/50 chance, and that night all the hell, filth, rejection, abandonment, hurt, pain, hatred, and everything else that I had been carrying from my past, showed up. And it showed up tremendously! I reacted horribly! I did things that I would have never done, and I certainly said things that I would have never said and things that I lived to regret! As disgusting as my own words and actions were, it needed to happen. I needed to get real with Abba about what was still in me, and I needed to be purged and cleansed. This is what I needed, and my life was dependent upon it. This incident allowed me to see *me* and to finally face the truth that I needed to be cleansed, for real! There was no mask that I could create that could cover this amount of pain from this type of betrayal.

Hurt people hurt people!

It is no cliché; It is the unadulterated Truth! Hurt people, hurt people the same way that Healed people, heal people! DJ and I both needed healing. He too needed healing from the wounds of his past. It is his story to tell not mine. I know that I wrote this with a focus on women, however, there are countless men and boys that are wounded and living stuck in the trauma of their pasts. I give all glory to Jesus for saving, healing, and delivering us both. We are still growing to be better. Not just for one another, but as individuals.

So, the unveiling, the exposing, and the purging was vital for me to get to this place. Remember when I said in the introduction that deliverance is not a walk in the park, nor is it pretty? I meant it. This place has been one hell of a journey to get to and I had to fight for and with my life. I had to fight for my daughter's life. And I had to fight to break every generational curse in my lineage. I had to die to everything in my past to be prepared for my future. As painful as it was to be exposed; to *get naked* in my truth, it was so liberating. And I was willing to do the work. I was willing to do the *heart work* which was the *hard work*. I was willing, before my liberty, to share my story, because it was in August of 2010 that I received the instruction from the Holy Spirit to write. I must be honest; I was petrified to share anything that had happened to me, the disgusting things that I had done, and my lifestyle of choice. I was too afraid of what people may think if they knew my truth. If they knew how dark and ugly my past was and if they knew the things that I still struggle with, would I be judged only to be rejected again? Would those that did claim to love me so much, suddenly abandon me? Would my transparency be too transparent? The answer to all these questions has been, yes! I would be rejected, judged, abandoned, and my transparency would be outright offensive to some. Quite a few have walked away without any explanation.

I used to get upset, cry, lose sleep, and question what I had done, and the spirit of depression would try to creep in again. Until I got a revelation that I had done nothing at all. I was always the one running back to make things right when others could care less if I even existed. Although it has been painful, and there have been times that I felt the sting, rejection no longer has a hold on me and I have learned, like Jesus, to shake the dust from my feet and keep it moving. Not in an arrogant way, but with the understanding that I have a Kingdom mandate on my life, and I will not be distracted. I am a terrorist to the kingdom of darkness, and I make no apologies for it. The anointing came with a heavy cost. You were not there when Jesus saved me. You were not there the night that I was in the strip club, high off cocaine and marijuana, five thousand dollars on the table, and He spoke to me, "Are you not worth more than four quarters?" YOU WERE NOT THERE! I paid for this OIL, and I will pour it out on My Jesus as often as I get the opportunity! I pray that you never be ashamed of the cost to carry what you carry!

It was also when I was walking through the darkness and valley experiences of 2013 and in my purging season that I asked God, "Why do I always end up getting hurt? Why do I always get handed a plate of shit and then told how to eat it? Why do I always have to forgive and kiss people's asses and they just walk all over me like a piece of trash or drop me like a used tissue when they have used me up?" His response, *"I forgave you."* Those three words were so powerful to me and gave me a freedom like no other. *I was forgiven!* Because I was forgiven, I had to forgive, but I did not know how. I had to be taught to forgive. I had to learn to pray for them and even for those that I had done wrong to. When I could pray for others and mourn for their souls in the same manner that I could mourn for mine, without any anger in my heart, but in pure love, I knew that I had learned to forgive.

I now utterly understand forgiveness. It has taken many years to get to this place, but I am so grateful that I made it. I have forgiven and set free every person in this story and many unnamed and never mentioned. Each of them, living or deceased from this life, helped to cultivate me in all areas of my growth. I understood when Bishop TD Jakes said that when he speaks, you are hearing from all those before him. (*Don't Drop the Mic: The Power of Your Words Can Change the World,* TD Jakes, 2021). Each person in my life has inspired me, equipped me, groomed me, encouraged, and empowered me, even in the worst of situations. I thank them! My mom, what a beautiful relationship we have now. It took nearly twenty-eight years for me to even have a conversation with her, but I thank Abba Father for redeeming the time and for mending our broken places. This precious lady received the unmerited gift of Salvation at the age of 64. HE IS A PROMISE KEEPER!

While walking out the forgiveness of my mother and my father and all my grandparents, the Words spoken by Holy Spirit, set me free. He said to me, concerning my mother, "She could only give you what had been given to her". PHEWWWW! She could only access the skills and the tools that she was given to become a woman and to be a mother. I could now make that same connection with my dad, my grandparents, my ex, and my husband. This is how I process forgiveness toward everyone now.

Once I had forgiven them and released them from the prison that I had built in my own heart, I could then begin the lifelong process to forgive myself and to continually fall in love with me and the woman that I am still becoming. I gave myself permission to fall in love with me the same way that Yahweh is in love with me.

"Some are lost in the fire. Some are built from it" ~Unknown

I shared my story with the hopes that if you or someone that you know, and love have had similar experiences that you would see *hope*. I shared because I know that there are hundreds of thousands, if not millions that have, are, or will, struggle with some of the exact same things, and I want them to see *hope*. I shared my story so that you would not think for a single moment that your past is any worse than mine. We ALL have a story. And we all have areas that we are still being healed and delivered in.

The purpose in the work of, *I Am Broken Beautiful* is to show you, my Beloveds, the overwhelming, relentless, unconditional, transformational Love of Yahweh through Yeshua. I share my Testimony to show you His goodness and His faithfulness and His mercy and what GRACE looks like in real life! Not some dressed up watered down version of me, but the ME that JESUS saw worthy to rescue! The version that is honest and raw, but never caused Him shame nor embarrassment!

The version that He would leave the 99 for! The version that He gave His life for and the version that He could "Trust with the Trouble" to fulfill His divine purpose in the Earth for such a time as this!

I choose to no longer live in the vicious cycles of past trauma, nor do I allow the residue of betrayal and manipulation cling to me. I choose to no longer produce nor welcome any unhealthy habits and patterns into my life that hinder my growth. I choose to no longer hold on to resentment and the bitterness of unforgiveness in my heart towards anyone, this includes myself. I choose to no longer be bound by the shackles of depression, and anxiety no longer has permission to have its nasty grip on my thoughts. Though there have been times, very recently, that I have been abandoned and have had people that I love deeply to just pull away and cut me off without warning or reason, the sting of it no longer has a lasting effect on me. Post-traumatic stress disorder no longer enslaves me with its web of deception, nightmares, and trigger points. Fear of failure, doubting my purpose, insecurities, people pleasing, and the lies that I would never be good enough, no longer have a voice. The spirit of suicide has been annihilated over my life, and I know that my life is worth living.

It was worth the crushing and the pressing and the beatings. It was worth all the pain and the suffering. It was all worth it to be *alive* and to be here with you today, and to be granted this life-changing opportunity to share my testimony with you. It was all worth it!

Holy Spirit spoke to one of my most Beloved sisters about a month ago concerning me, so she shared with me the Words that were spoken.

"There is nothing that Tasha has been through that has been in vain. There is nothing that was lost. Because she suffered with Me, she will Reign with Me."

So, Beloved, again, it was all worth it! To have a relationship restored with my mom, to be able to break generational curses in my lineage and to leave a legacy for my children's children. I am still believing that every relationship in my family circle is made new.

Beloved, my prayer for you is that now that you have read the words of this work that your heart is moved with compassion, your Spirit is awakened within you and that you have a desire to seek the heart and the arms of Your Savior, Jesus Christ!

I pray that you feel His love and His Anointing drawing you into intimacy with Him. I pray that, if you have not, that you ask Jesus to take the heavy burdens of your heart and teach you to lay them down at His feet. Whether it be mental dis-ease, pain from your past or things that you may be facing now. If it is people that you are still holding hostage in the prison that you have built, or even if it is you that you have yet to give permission to be free, I pray that happens for you now. I pray that you feel the arms of Jesus wrapped around you, holding you and drawing you close to His bosom, so close that you begin to hear His heartbeat. I pray that ministering Angels begin to whisper to you just how much that you are loved and that you are safe and that your healing and deliverance begins in this very moment. I pray that you see His Face on and through the words on the pages and that His presence permeates within your heart and home from this day forward like you have never encountered. I pray that you know that there is nothing that you may have done, has ever been done to you, nor anything that you may do in the future that would ever stop Him from coming after you. I pray that you know that your brokenness, no matter how shattered, is beautiful in the hands of the Creator. You are loved by Love!

There is a passage of Scripture that comes to my mind as I am writing, and I pray that you are blessed to the overflow with its revelation as I was. It is found at Mark 5: 25-30 & vs. 34 (Amp)...

"And there was a woman who had a flow of blood for twelve years, and who had endured much suffering under the hands of many physicians and had spent all that she had, and was no better but instead grew worse. She had heard the reports

concerning Jesus, and she had came up behind Him in the throng and touched His garment, For she kept saying, 'If I only touch His garments, I shall be restored to health'. And immediately her flow of blood dried up at the source, and suddenly she felt in her body that she was healed of her distressing ailment. And Jesus, recognizing, in Himself, that the power proceeding from Him had gone forth, turned around immediately in the crowd and said, 'Who touched my clothes?' And He said to her, 'Daughter, your faith (your trust and confidence in me, springing from your faith in God) has restored you to health. Go into peace and be continually healed and freed from your distressing bodily disease'."

When she heard *about* Jesus, it freed her from her suffering! But, when she heard *from* Jesus, it freed her from her shame! How long have you suffered and lived under the labels that the enemy has placed on you? I tell you today, just like the "woman with the issue of blood" as we have all heard her called every time her story has ever been told, you have been called by your identity... Daughter! Just like her, it was not what He *told* her, it is what He *called* her...Daughter! No longer are you a label. You are His Daughter! No longer are you the victim nor the villain of your past. You are His Daughter! You can, just like her, find yourself at your wits end, and say within yourself, "If I may but touch the garment of Jesus, I will be made whole".

Again, my heartfelt prayer for you is that you make the decision to no longer live a life stained with defeat. That you no longer allow the voices of your past to scream louder than your present and your divine purpose, because as soon as you do, you will begin to see the beauty coming forth from your brokenness and everything divinely connected to you will flourish. There is a beautiful "After This" awaiting you. I promise and Jesus is here to hold your hand and walk you through it.

There is nothing too dirty that He cannot make worthy. He washed me in mercy. I Am Clean.

I Am Broken Beautiful...

ABOUT THE *Author*

TASHA RENE'E

Author Tasha Rene'e

Tasha is a mommy and an ordained Evangelist, published author, Founder and CEO of Broken Beautiful, LLC, where she serves not only as an accredited licensed Transformational Life Coach, she is also a certified Christian Mentor. As a Transformational Life Coach, she supports, inspires, empowers and encourages women that are ready to transition from Broken to Beautiful.

She is also the Visionary of S.H.I.F.T - *Sisters Healing In Faith Together* Women's Life Group where she teaches and demonstrates to women their value according to GOD's Holy Word.

Before Tasha understood who she is, embraced who she is created to be, and live the life she is destined to live, Tasha was Broken. She was broken by "life". She had suffered abuse, abandonment, rejection, and was severely misused. She lived a life in a vicious cycle of Survival.

In 2013 Tasha was clinically diagnosed with depression and Post Traumatic Stress Disorder (PTSD), and in 2010 she was hospitalized due to the weight and the paralyzing grip of anxiety. She, unfortunately, knows all too well the residue and the damage that unhealed brokenness from trauma leaves behind. She also knows well what it's like to create unhealthy relationships searching for validation and self-worth.

Because of these things, there was a relentless desperation to be healed and set free from the bondage of her past and she was willing to do the "heart" work that it took not only to be healed for herself, but so that she could walk with others on their healing journey.

"In every facet of my life and Ministry, my Divine Purpose is to help women that are or were just like me, to know that you too are Broken Beautiful and there is an amazing "After This" waiting just on the other side. So, when you make the decision to stop accepting a life of defeat,

stop allowing the voices of your past to scream louder than your Purpose and Finally stand in the TRUTH OF YOUR OWN BEAUTIFUL... Everything that you are connected to will Flourish"
~Tasha Renée

5 For I,' declares the Lord, 'will be a wall of fire around her [protecting her from enemies], and I will be the glory in her midst.'" Zechariah 2:5 and 10 (Amplified Bible)

Website: www.IAmBrokenBeautiful.com
Email: BrokenBeautifulTJ@gmail.com / CoachTJ@IAmBrokenBeautiful.com
Facebook: Tasha Jones
Instagram: @IAmBrokenBeautiful

Thank You For Your Support

getpublished@sheropublishing.com

SHEROPUBLISHING.COM

Made in the USA
Las Vegas, NV
31 July 2021

27272466R00085